THE BOY IN THE BUBBLE

Mark Patrick Hederman is Abbot of Glenstal Abbey, a Benedictine monastery in Co. Limerick, Ireland. A former headmaster of Glenstal Abbey School, his doctorate was in the philosophy of education. He studied philosophy and theology in Paris, with a special interest in Emmanuel Levinas. From 1976 to 1984, he edited with Richard Kearney *The Crane Bag Journal of Irish Studies*. He is author of ten books since the turn of the century, including *I Must be Talking to Myself* (Veritas, 2004), *Symbolism* (Veritas, 2007) and *Dancing with Dinosaurs* (Columba, 2011).

MARK PATRICK HEDERMAN

THE BOY IN THE BUBBLE

EDUCATION AS PERSONAL RELATIONSHIP

VERITAS

Published 2012 by
Veritas Publications
7–8 Lower Abbey Street
Dublin 1
publications@veritas.ie
www.veritas.ie

ISBN 978 1 84730 405 6

10 9 8 7 6 5 4 3 2 1

'St Kevin and the Blackbird' by Seamus Heaney © 1996
is reprinted by kind permission of Faber and Faber Ltd.

Cover design by Emmaus O'Herlihy, Glenstal Abbey
Typesetting by Colette Dower, Veritas Publications
Printed in the Republic of Ireland by
Hudson Killeen Ltd, Dublin

Veritas books are printed on paper made from the wood pulp of managed forests. For every tree felled, at least one tree is planted, thereby renewing natural resources.

To Celestine Cullen OSB, born in 1927, the year that Glenstal Abbey was founded; student at Glenstal Abbey School from 1939 to 1945; headmaster of Glenstal Abbey School from 1961 to 1975; Abbot of Glenstal Abbey from 1980 to 1992; Abbot President of the Benedictine Congregation of the Annunciation from 1992 to 2004.

Happy indeed is the man
Whose delight is the law of the Lord
And who ponders his law day and night.
He is like a tree that is planted
Beside the flowing waters,
That yields its fruit in due season
And whose leaves shall never fade;
And all that he does shall prosper.

Psalm 1

CONTENTS

PREFACE
9

INTRODUCTION
11

CHAPTER ONE
Education and the Deathly Hallows
15

CHAPTER TWO
Moses, Macbeth and Madame Montessori
31

CHAPTER THREE
Imagination in Education
43

CHAPTER FOUR
Education as Personal Relationship
55

CHAPTER FIVE
Pat Clarke and Paulo Freire
69

CHAPTER SIX
Mythic Intelligence
95

CHAPTER SEVEN
Music in Numbers
109

CHAPTER EIGHT
Alexander Pushkin in Ireland
121

CHAPTER NINE
Cherishing and Challenging
139

CHAPTER TEN
Father de Pradts and Miss Jean Brodie
149

CHAPTER ELEVEN
The Special Humility of the Educator
161

CHAPTER TWELVE
Glenstal Abbey School
169

CONCLUSION
195

PREFACE

David Phillip Vetter, a boy from Texas, was born with a genetic disease known as severe combined immunodeficiency (SCID). This required him to live almost his entire life in a sterilised, bubble-shaped cocoon at the Texas Children's Hospital in Houston, to 'isolate' him from germs and viruses. His condition made him famous in the media, where he was known as 'the boy in the bubble'. David died on 22 February 1984, aged twelve. The bubble-shaped isolation unit in which he lived, created by NASA at the Johnson Space Center, can be seen at the Smithsonian National Museum of American History. Vetter's tragic life and death brought up many ethical issues about the viability of isolation treatment. Fortunately, advances in medicine over the years have rendered such treatment obsolete.

However, David's condition might be thought of as ours writ large. Martin Buber's intuition about each one of us as human beings is that we are born individuals inside a mobile biological isolation system, and that we only become persons by releasing ourselves from this solitary confinement and developing what he called an 'I-Thou' relationship with someone outside our individuality orbit. Becoming a person, to Buber, means stepping outside the isolation unit into which we are born as individuals, and extending ourselves into the surrounding space between ourselves and others. This space 'in between' is the habitat of persons.

We all live in a 'bubble' when it comes to meeting other people and the world we are required to inhabit. We self-protect from all such contact by surrounding ourselves with a shell, and we have to find ways to stretch out into the world around us, like snails emerging into sunlight. There are several methods of developing this special relationship – one of these is through education.

There is, in Buber's view, a particular I-Thou educational relationship. This is the specific task of all genuine educators, and any other kind of learning is secondary to, and dependent upon, this primary undertaking. Education means leading individuals out into the space of personhood. This is the hallowed charge placed in the hands of those entrusted with the education of others. If they do justice to their calling they will be responsible for the miracle of personhood in our world; if they betray this trust they can do damage to those in their care, making it almost impossible for them ever to become persons. So demanding, so necessary and so daunting is this task that it requires complete understanding of the specific relationship for which we are responsible.

INTRODUCTION

Your children are not your children.
They are the sons and daughters of Life's longing for itself.
They come through you but not from you,
And though they are with you yet they belong not to you.

You may give them your love but not your thoughts,
For they have their own thoughts.
You may house their bodies but not their souls,
For their souls dwell in the house of tomorrow,
which you cannot visit, not even in your dreams.
You may strive to be like them, but seek not to make them like
    you.
For life goes not backward nor tarries with yesterday.
You are the bows from which your children as living arrows are
    sent forth.

The Archer sees the mark upon the path of the infinite, and He
    bends you with His might that His arrows may go swift and
    far.
Let your bending in the Archer's hand be for gladness;
For even as He loves the arrow that flies, so He loves also the
    bow that is stable.

– Kahlil Gibran, The Prophet

The great dilemma for those of us involved in education is that we are trying to prepare our children for a world that we will never know and can never enter. Every generation is a new world never before explored by humankind. And yet we have to prepare those who are destined to inhabit this new territory for the task ahead of them. How should we do this? The worst possible way is to pretend that tomorrow's world will be the same as today's, and that the skills, the virtues and the values which we used to cope will be appropriate or sufficient to allow our children to survive and to thrive in the strange horizon which is rising up to meet them. Certainly memory will not be enough; imagination and creativity will be their most important helpmates. Teaching them what we learned, in the way we learnt it, will be as useful to them as swordplay and musketry in nuclear warfare. We have to be humble and realistic about our capacities to educate. Our children, for all we know, may someday be living on the moon, and preparing them for life on Sunnydale Farm is not doing them any favours. And yet we have to do something. They have to spend time with us while they are growing up and achieving their independence, and we have to develop some programme for their education until they finally leave the nest and strike out on their own.

Ireland, as a small independent country with a comparatively small number of children, should be able to devise a way of educating that is wholesome and inspiring. Finland can act as an example of a small country blessed with an exceptional flowering of musical genius. They have learned from their experience of such riches and have put educational opportunities for musical talent in place that put the rest of us to shame. After the break-up of the Soviet Union in the early 1990s, Finland experienced a severe recession, not dissimilar to current difficulties in Ireland. The Finnish government of the day bravely decided that increased investment in education was the roadmap to recovery. The result? Finland emerged quickly from recession, built a highly skilled workforce, and today boasts one of the finest education systems in the world.

The purpose of this book is to question how we move in such a direction. Even if you disagree with everything I say in these pages, they may perhaps provoke you into articulating the educational structures that both of us would be happy to see in place. Education, by its very nature, is always arbitrary and pragmatic, no matter how profound and well-intentioned the philosophy behind it. In most schools, day-to-day practicalities require making it up as we go along. There is always someone absent, always some unforeseen crisis, always something that doesn't work. And yet the children arrive and they have to be looked after.

Education is nearly always mediocre and disobliging. If you are a substitute teacher and you ask the class what they have been learning from the teacher you replace, they will say that they have learned nothing and that their teacher is hopeless. And when you leave the class you can be quite sure that they will say the same about you. And yet the day goes on and the hours on the timetable inexorably unfold. The way this happens depends upon how enlightened and how committed we are. Most of us are too lazy to work it out for ourselves, so we fall back upon what we hope are tried and trusted ways of keeping them occupied.

Educational structures are always out of date. They were put in place by previous generations. Ours are mostly from the nineteenth century with a few gewgaws and gadgets thrown in to give an impression of being state-of-the-art. Most schools with great reputations live on the kudos of charismatic educators long since departed. Everything in education is yesterday's news because the problems and the pitfalls 'at the chalkface' of today (if anyone still uses chalk) haven't yet reached public consciousness. We keep on saying it to ourselves until it has become a cliché: education is for the whole person. But who or what is the 'whole person'? Have you ever met one? Has there ever been one?

CHAPTER ONE

Education and the Deathly Hallows

> That which Voldemort does not value, he takes no trouble to understand. Of house-elves and children's tales, of love, loyalty, and innocence, Voldemort knows and understands nothing. Nothing. That they all have a power beyond his own, a power beyond the reach of any magic, is a truth he has never grasped.[1]

For the most part, we are a mystery to ourselves. We live our lives in a small area of artificial light which we call consciousness. We choose to live and move in our day-to-day world within this orbit. But there is a vast area beyond this which we have learned to call the unconscious, simply because we have no idea about it. We were not always aware of it, and only very recently have we recognised how important it is, not only to acknowledge that it exists but also to try to integrate it as much as possible into the way we run our lives. It is now a century since we discovered this reality about ourselves and yet, we have to admit, our systems of education have hardly changed at all from the times before the discovery was made.

In Ireland we have made little or no effort to cater for this reality. It is as if the ship we are sailing on became our complete universe, without reference to the ocean on which it was floating. European culture, and particularly Irish culture since the foundation of this state as an independent entity, has been constructed over this ocean. However, as we have discovered comparatively recently, the reality below has

---

[1] J. K. Rowling, *Harry Potter and the Deathly Hallows* (New York: Arthur A. Levine Books, 2007), p. 710.

festered from neglect. The ideals, on which we based the conduct of our lives and upon which we structured our systems of education, are hybrid and ancient, coming as they do from European philosophy. They are very noble. They have inspired the geometry of Euclid, the Empire State Building, the Gothic cathedrals of Europe. But the trouble is that they are not *us*. We are made up of both the conscious and unconscious.

Whatever the reasons, resistance to acknowledgement of the unconscious aspect of ourselves was particularly trenchant and totalitarian towards the end of the nineteenth and the first half of the twentieth century. In this stubborn refusal to accept the full reality of our common humanity, there was little to choose between Victorian England and Catholic Ireland. However, it was in such an antagonistic climate that twentieth-century Europe and North America became both the time and the place of the 'discovery' of this subcontinent and the locus of the reaping of its whirlwind.

Discovery of the 'unconscious' was as world-shattering as the European discovery of America in 1492. It revealed that the world we knew was only a part of the whole reality, most of which was subterranean. We had to reinvent our map of the world. This new dimension made most of what we had thought about the world up to that date anachronistic. We had been living on the top storey of a house with a vast cellar underneath and we had only now been given a key to the trapdoor leading down into its uninvestigated depths.

Many of us are now aware that the twentieth century was a hell on earth for most of its inhabitants, apart from the privileged few who were mostly white male plutocrats. This hell on earth, we have also come to realise, was a human invention. It was a hell of cruelty and mayhem resulting from the incapacity of powerful people to decipher their unconscious motivation, whether in concentration camps, penal institutions, families or schools.

After the Holocaust there should be no possibility of neglecting the unconscious. Such investigation is no longer a luxury or an optional extra. It has become mandatory, Whatever is not made conscious is likely to be repeated. One of the major obstacles to dealing with this reality in an effective way is the refusal to admit that it exists at all, or the conviction that it is unnecessary to find out about it and integrate it into our psychological, our social, our educated selves. The first task of our educational objective must be to allow our children to become aware of the unconscious side of themselves and to provide them with the wherewithal to cope with this reality. Introducing ourselves to the unconscious means listening to it and allowing it to inform us of its presence.

In 1909, Freud and Jung were in America for seven weeks on a lecture tour. While there they analysed each other's dreams. Jung's most important dream was one of the causes of his break with Freud and one of his own most important contributions to psychoanalysis. He dreamt that he was on the top floor of an old house, which was very elegant and well furnished, and he marvelled at the possibility that this could be his own house. And then he realised that he had only visited the upper storey and had no idea what the lower floor was like, so he decided to explore. He found everything underneath much older. And after a while he noticed that the stone slabs of this lower floor were moveable. There was also an iron ring attached to one of them. He was able to use the ring to move the slab and reveal a narrow stone stairway, which descended further. He went down these stairs and lowered himself into a cave cut out of rock. Bones and pottery were scattered in the dust, along with two human skulls half-disintegrated.

Freud and Jung offered different interpretations of this dream. For Jung it became the template of his version of psychoanalysis. The house was an image of the psyche. The room on the upper floor was our day-to-day conscious personality. As he moved downwards, the lower floor was the first level of the unconscious, which he thought of as our personal unconscious. The area unveiled by loosening the stone slabs on the ground floor was what he called the collective unconscious. Jung believed that he had unearthed the world of the most primitive levels of our psyche, our common heritage as human beings, shaped by all our ancestors. He invented the term 'archetype' to describe the decipherable elements that make up at least part of this vast uncharted area. Archetypes are like the slides that we project from the unconscious upon the walls of the conscious world we inhabit. They give us some indication of the nature of the unconscious and the machinery that creates and projects them. Jung discovered that archetypes were 'identical psychic structures common to all' and made up 'the archaic heritage of humanity'.[2] In other words, they give us some clue of the make-up of the unconscious and some handle on how to cope with it. The archetypes spring from innate psychic mechanisms which, whether we like it or not, instigate, manipulate and operate our reactions to most typical human experience. For the most part, we think we are reacting towards various situations we find ourselves in with originality; but we find, according to Jung, that we are programmed archetypally to enact a series of predictable reactions, over which we have much less control than we credit ourselves with. This also means that on certain occasions, archetypes evoke similar reactions in terms of thoughts, images, symbols and feelings, in any or every person of whatever sex, class, creed or race, no matter when or where they lived on the planet. We are controlled by archetypal machinery in ways that take considerable effort to detect and to detonate.

An archetype is, therefore, one of the 'primordial, structural elements of the human psyche'. It is there in all of us and is present in all peoples and societies in history.

---

[2] Carl G. Jung, III 'The Transformation of Libido' and IV 'The Origin of the Hero', *Symbols of Transformation*, Part II, *Collected Works*, Vol. 5, Bollingen Series XX (New York: Pantheon, 1956), #224, #259.

Literature and dreams record examples of this universal phenomenon. The archetype of the child is one of the ever-recurring motifs in individual dreams, as well as in world mythology and literature. It represents the potential future both of each one of us and of our societies. It symbolises the whole personality in its development. For Jung, '[t]he mythic child symbolises the lifelong process of psychological maturation'.[3] Like all archetypes, it is bipolar, with both a positive and a negative aspect. The positive side appears as the Divine Child who represents newness, potential for growth, hope for the future. The negative side is the child who refuses to grow up and meet the challenges of life. Jung says that when we dream of a child it usually heralds or contains the solution to some crisis in our lives. The child in our dream represents the third term, which we are unable to conjure up in our day-to-day attempts to solve the problem in which we are embroiled. The child appearing in our dream is like the avatar heralding the arrival of an as-yet-unheard-of solution. The child in the dream gives hope for the discovery of some new element, which will break the deadlock of whatever impasse is causing our unconscious to react. What is true for individuals in their dreams is true for whole societies in their myths and in their legends. We have to examine such manifestations from the unconscious, especially at the beginning of a new century, to achieve a comprehensive survey of the way we should go.

Jung's most sustained analysis of the child archetype provides the basis of what I say here.[4] The child archetype is an example of such primordial images found in myths, fairytales and psychotic fantasies as well as in dreams. Products of the unconscious may be divided into two categories: fantasies of a personal nature, which can be traced

---

[3] Robert A. Segal, *Theorizing About Myth* (Amherst: University of Massachusetts Press, 1999), p. 84.
[4] C. G. Jung, 'The Psychology of the Child Archetype', *The Archetypes and the Collective Unconscious,* Part IV, *Collected Works,* Vol. 9i, Bollingen Series XX, #259 to #305.

to repression by the individual; and fantasies of an impersonal nature, not individually acquired, which correspond to inherited collective elements of the human psyche. This second category can be called the collective unconscious. Such unconscious material can enter consciousness while we are in a state of reduced awareness, such as in dream, when the control of the unconscious by the conscious mind is lessened.

Archetypes are living psychic forces which can promote human growth if understood and incorporated into our lives but which, when neglected, may cause negative reactions. We would do well to carefully examine such signs of the times as we advance through the first quarter of a new century, because messages from the unconscious that occur in works of art and literature can help us to negotiate our passage more successfully. We neglect them at our peril.

The role of the archetype in our psychic structure is to represent or personify certain instinctive data from the unconscious. We must live with the manifestation for as long as it takes to crack its code and benefit from what it is trying to reveal. Too hasty an attempt to understand and domesticate it could bypass its essential meaning altogether. These instinctive forces in our make-up are usually so foreign to us that we need to make considerable adjustment to our normal ways of procedure to allow ourselves to hear fully their cry. However, such information is vital to us if we are to cater satisfactorily for what we are as complete human beings. It is also of huge import in our attempts to prepare our children for satisfactory and fulfilling lives in the world they are about to inherit.

The function of the child archetype is to appear from the unconscious as a warning. It represents that other side of ourselves which has been neglected in our perfectly understandable attempt to improve our lot and to get ahead.

The child who appears in our dreams tries to compensate for or correct the inevitable one-sidedness and extravagance of the conscious mind in its ideological attempt to construct the best of all possible worlds. The child archetype tries to remind us of all those other realities and sides of ourselves which we have left out in the often somewhat myopic programme of well-being which we have constructed. Archetypal dreams and stories are the natural result of too much conscious concentration on a few aspects to the exclusion of all others. Since the child is essentially a potential being, the child motif signifies anticipation of a future which can pave the way for change that might satisfy more comprehensively the full reality of what we really are. As a figure, the archetypal child represents the future development of ourselves as human beings. This appearance of the child may be in the form of a god or a hero. Their arrival is often associated with miraculous birth and early struggles and adversities. Such universal themes of insignificant beginnings and miraculous birth represent the emergence of a new and as-yet-unknown future from a somewhat squalid and monotonous present reality.

Experiences in our conscious life and our present existence, of conflict from which there is no conceivable means of escape, are what cause the unconscious to create a third presence of an irrational nature, which the conscious mind neither expects nor understands. Such is the symbolic emergence of the child figure. The child in our dreams or in literature represents a moving towards independence. This usually requires the added symbol of abandonment as a necessary precondition for the detachment of the child from its origins or from anything that might be connected with the imprisoning circumstances in which we find ourselves. The symbol of the child anticipates a new higher state of consciousness, which may remain a mythological projection if it is not actually integrated into our plans for the future. The typical fates of the child figures as they occur in our dreams or as they are related in our stories are symbols of events that occur during our struggles and our progress toward wholeness. The child personifies the most vital urge to realise the self, and as such has great power. Although the child of our dreams and of our stories is often delivered into hazardous situations and is in continual danger of extinction, he or she possesses supernatural powers far beyond the human. The invincibility of this child is the measure of our determination to press on into the future and to achieve the ultimate goal of wholeness for our humanity.

Most of us think the greatest possible achievement is to come up with everything ourselves, to invent and be creative, put our stamp on the world. But there are those who consider that the greater achievement is to listen, to change this world by bringing into it what no one else is able to hear. Into the humdrum and ordinary they bring something extraordinary, a magic. This magic is usually the product of our unconscious and comes about through listening carefully to what our unconscious is trying to whisper to us. Like dreams, most significant art comes from the unconscious and is filtered through the genius of particularly gifted artists. Such works appear 'out of the blue' as symptoms of our current malaise and as signposts towards a possible escape route.

When someone dreams up a child, or children, which a whole generation of our children spontaneously recognise and adopt as their mascot, then we have to sit up and take notice because here we may have a dream of, or for, our future.

We might present the character of Harry Potter as an example of such a heroic child archetype for the twenty-first century. The seven fantasy novels in which he features chronicle the adventures of the child wizard and his friends. Huge numbers of children, and adults, all over the world have had Harry Potter and his friends as their most important guides throughout their childhood. The series has sold about 450 million copies to date and has been translated into sixty-seven languages; the last four consecutively set records as the fastest-selling books in history, making the *Harry Potter* brand worth in excess of $15 billion.

A friend of mine was in China recently. He had the privilege of meeting several groups of primary school children in schools. He asked the children, through an interpreter, what books they were reading. They said *Harry Potter*. All of which shows the collective archetype into which the author, J. K. Rowling, has inserted herself and her hero.

Are we dealing here with sterling or with straw? Can 450 million book buyers be wrong? Harold Bloom, Sterling Professor of Humanities at Yale, says, 'Yes, they can be wrong!' In a, by now, infamous review for the *Wall Street Journal*, Bloom recognises that 'Rowling ... is at least a millennial index to our popular culture.' But this, according to him, is more a reflection on us than on her. *Harry Potter*, for Bloom, represents the dumbing down of global readership everywhere. Rowling is preparing our children to spend the rest of their lives reading Stephen King! 'So huge an audience,' says the horrified professor, 'gives her importance akin to rock stars, movie idols, TV anchors, and successful politicians. Her prose style, heavy on cliché, makes no demands upon her readers.'[5] In other words, *Harry Potter* is the ultimate brain candy for twenty-first-century morons.

A. S. Byatt, herself a Booker-prize-winning novelist, agrees with Bloom:

> It is written for people whose imaginative lives are confined to TV cartoons, and the exaggerated (more exciting, not threatening) mirror-worlds of soaps, reality TV and celebrity gossip. She speaks to an adult generation that hasn't known, and doesn't care about, mystery.[6]

To quote Doris Egan, 'Byatt implies that the Potter books are pasteurized-processed cheez-food and that the adults

---

[5] Harold Bloom, 'Can 35 Million Book Buyers Be Wrong? Yes', *Wall Street Journal* (11 July 2000).
[6] *New York Times* (7 June 2003).

reading them are too dim to tell the difference between them and the fare of a four-star chef'.[7]

This is a constant phenomenon in the world of so-called experts. They keep on telling us what they think we should be doing, rather than telling us the meaning of what we prefer to do. They slam films or books we love, not because of what they are in themselves, but because they are not what these critics think they should be. Complaining that Rowling is not Tolkien, that *Harry Potter* is not *The Hobbit*, is as helpful as telling us that surf boards are not submarines. Of course they're not: they were meant to be, and to do, completely different things.

If we at least agree that the Potter books make up part of a genre which we can describe as 'fantasy novels', then we can begin to identify the place they occupy on the library shelves of world literature. There is an ancestry of fantasy books as varied and as weighty as any other literary tradition, against which *Harry Potter* has to be measured. But there are different species within this category itself.

There is 'high fantasy' and 'low fantasy', with a ladder of gradation between the two. High and low in this instance are positions on a scale and not value judgements. High fantasy is set in an alternative, entirely fictional world distinct from the real, or everyday, world. This 'secondary' world which fantasy creates is internally consistent but its rules differ from those of the 'primary' world in which most of us live. Low fantasy, on the other hand, is set in our primary, or 'real' world, which then is allowed to include magical elements.

Tolkien, C. S. Lewis and J. K. Rowling can illustrate three descending steps on this ladder from high to low fantasy. Tolkien's fiction creates a world of its own and provides detailed maps, a geography and a history of this fictional

---

[7] Doris Egan, 'For They Will Say Both Yes and No (a reply to A. S. Byatt's critique of *Harry Potter*)', www.dorisegan.com/essays/for-they-will-say-both-yes-and-no-a-reply-to-a-s-byatts-critique-of-harry-potter/

world to help us negotiate it. Lewis moves us into a world parallel to this one through portals from our own. Narnia, for instance, can be accessed through a wardrobe that exists in our ordinary, everyday world. Rowling's series represents low fantasy, or, as I prefer to think of it, 'sacramental fantasy': a presentation of our world after the incarnation, after the definitive entry of God into this, our primary world. These books present us with a distinct world-within-a-world. The structures of our familiar world remain in place, but within these structures strange things happen.

These stories are part and parcel of the primary world in which we all live. The inner world which they evoke provides the magic which should be an integral part of the world in which we live. It is another world within this one, although most of the mundane inhabitants of our primary world are unaware of it. This is also what St John describes in his Gospel: 'He was in the world (*en to kosmo*), and though the world (*ho kosmos*) was created through him, the world (*ho kosmos*) did not know him' (Jn 1:10). In one sentence you get three different nuances with regard to the word 'world.' The first use of *kosmos* refers to the physical realm into which Jesus Christ has entered. The second refers to the created order for which he is responsible as the Word of God; the third refers to the 'muggle-world', or the world of those who fail to recognise him.

As Doris Egan explains, *Harry Potter* fits into the fantasy map as something of 'a missing puzzle piece':

> These books don't make you fall to your knees — you're having too much fun to do that. They may freak you out from time to time, and there will be monsters; but they will restore the world we know at the end ... It's not high-church magic, but it's good enough magic for everyday wear; not numinous, but full of high spirits, in every sense of the word. And therefore 'ersatz' strikes me as a massively unfair word; it implies that something is passing for something else

— that the Potter books are trying to be numinous
fantasy and failing. And I don't think they're trying at
all. They're an entirely different species.[8]

Byatt and Bloom ignore the incarnational tradition of magic
books.

J. K. Rowling, like Charles Dickens, is an archetypal
storyteller – she tells it as it comes out of our collective
unconscious. All such stories wear local costume, though
they reach down to the depths, where they connect with the
global network of universal experience. Although the details
may be particular, the storyline is typical – anyone in the
world can relate to it.

Archetypal stories are ones to which all of us can relate
simply because we happen to be human beings. There are
two basic archetypal stories underpinning the mythology of
our Graeco-Roman and our Judeo-Christian culture: the
Odyssey and the Exodus, the journey and the escape. In
Homer's version, of course, they are all wearing sandals and
togas, but in Joyce's twentieth-century *Ulysses* the same
archetypal journey is situated in Dublin on 16 June 1904.
These details are irrelevant; it is the journey that matters to
all of us and in all of us. We have all moved from one place
to another, even if it was simply a day's excursion to the
seaside; thus we relate to archetypal stories of a journey: *Star
Trek* or *Wanderly Wagon* are basically the same story, even
though the first travels through the galaxy and the second
through the Irish countryside. Whether our journey is from
the nursery to the dining room or from Mars to Venus, they
are still recognisable as such.

As for the Exodus, *The Great Escape* is not just Steve
McQueen's story, it's my story and your story and
everybody's story. Moses, Pharaoh, the pillar and the cloud,
the Red Sea, the plagues, the desert and the Promised Land
– we've seen them all via Metro-Goldwyn-Mayer, who have

---

[8] Ibid.

been tuning into our archetypes into big-screen adventures for most of the last century. But let's not forget the network in ours psyches into which they plug their wares, Because we have all escaped from somewhere – from the nursery, from the family, from our school or from our job – so we can relate to *The Count of Monte Cristo*, Alexander Dumas' great saga which captured the imagination of the world. This archetypal story has been borrowed and transformed into plays, musicals, films and TV series the world over. In 1994, a Stephen King novella, *Rita Hayworth and Shawshank Redemption*, was made into a film voted by many as their favourite of all time. Andy Dufresne is sentenced to two consecutive life sentences at Shawshank State Penitentiary for murdering his wife and her lover. He is later assigned to the prison library, where he can be protected from bullying and use his exceptional banking skills to help the guards and the inmates of the prison. The very first book he puts into the library is *The Count of Monte Cristo*, which is both an acknowledgement of, and a reference to, the film's source.

Harry Potter is another such archetypal story. Potter is an orphan who discovers at the age of eleven that he is a magician who is living in a world of non-magical people, or 'muggles'. Harry's ability is inborn and such children are invited to attend a school that teaches the necessary skills to succeed in the world where magic is present. All our children are born with such innate magic in their blood and have the right to attend schools where it is cultivated and promoted. Unfortunately, in the muggle world in which we live, anyone who does happen to detect the working of imagination in any child will see to it that the Ministry of Magic [in our case read Ministry of Education] sends 'Obliviators' to cast memory charms upon such children – causing them to forget the wonderful gift they were displaying so naturally at the beginning of their school life.

In the first year at his 'privileged' school, Harry begins to explore the magical world and goes in quest of the Philosopher's Stone, which can be used to brew an elixir that can make the drinker immortal. This, of course, should be the quest of all children, but in the world of muggledom it is wiped off the desktop of every child who is required to get ahead. The person who tries to thwart Harry and all the children at Hogwart's school is Lord Voldemort, someone who wishes death instead of life on everyone with whom he comes in contact. 'Voldemort' is simply a synonym for what Eric Fromm defined as 'necrophilia' in his 1963 pamphlet 'War Within Man'.[9] There Fromm contrasts the healthy 'biophiliac' character orientation, which is open to life, growth, change and the future, with the unhealthy 'necrophiliac' character, which dwells in the past and attempts to render the world static, fixed, predictable and dead. The necrophiliac personality fears life because of its messiness, its randomness, its uncontrollability. And so they do their best to control it through brute force, fear, torture and ultimately death. Many institutions today could be described as 'necrophiliac'. We can recognise this in so many of the people who run and ruin our world. No matter what their political, religious or ideological affiliations, they worship strength and lack of feeling; they glorify the mechanical, doing their best to become machines themselves. Their obsessive fear, and compulsive need to control that fear, affects everybody around them, especially those who refuse to submit to their control.

To counteract the death-obsessed tendencies of the world around him, Harry joins the Order of the Phoenix, which is the bird of resurrection who rises from the ashes. Dumbledore, the head of Hogwarts School, is something of a loveable old fumbler who has his heart in the right place but who mistrusts his own judgement and wishes that he didn't have the onerous task of educating the magicians of tomorrow. There can be no fanatical know-alls in charge of

---

[9] 'War Within Man: A Psychological Inquiry into the Roots of Destructiveness. A Study and Commentary' was a pre-publication of Fromm's concept of biophilia and necrophilia as it was later published in 1964's *The Heart of Man* (London: HarperCollins, 1980).

anybody's future. On the other hand, the great adversary to growth and fulfilment for the children at the school is Draco Malfoy. *Mal foi* means 'bad faith' in French and was a favourite term used by Jean-Paul Sartre and Simone de Beauvoir to describe *mauvaise foi*, where a human being under pressure from societal forces adopts false values and disowns their innate freedom to act.

Throughout all the novels in the series, Harry Potter struggles with the difficulties of adolescence coupled with the onus of being a famous wizard. Following Dumbledore's death, Voldemort completes his ascension to power and gains control of the Ministry of Magic. With the death-dealer in charge of education, Harry, Ron and Hermione leave Hogwarts to hunt and destroy Voldemort's remaining Horcruxes – objects containing parts of a person's soul. The Hallows and the Horcruxes of 'education' are not the vision statements or the people behind them, they are the historical circumstances which surround us and which dictate the ways in which such propaganda is implemented. And, more importantly, they are the perceptions of the contemporary population, especially parents, about what they consider to be the criteria of success for their children. What the people think and what the media portray are quite different from the project as outlined by the various philosophers of education behind the scenes.

Many conservative Christian parents refuse to allow their children to read the Potter stories, claiming that they promote witchcraft and wickedness. Pastor Jack Brock of Christ Community Church in Alamogordo, New Mexico, had a holy bonfire on the Sunday after Christmas 2001, and burnt the Potter books publicly as 'an abomination to God and to me'. Richard Abanes, in *Harry Potter and The Bible*, shows a direct link with 'current paganism' and the practice of witchcraft, as well as ties to the occult and new-age philosophy. Connie Neal's *What's a Christian to do with Harry Potter?* has a chapter entitled: 'What would Jesus do with *Harry Potter*?' The Potter mythology, as well as having classical allusions (described by Elizabeth Schafer in *Exploring Harry Potter*) is also steeped in the Christian tradition which spawned both the author and her hero:

> The simple fact is, the only newness about Rowling's fictional world is the freshness with which she treats old themes and invents new ones. The world of magic and miracle has been around for a long, long time, and is an intrinsic part of the Judeo–Christian heritage, whatever explanations conservative Christians may wish to offer for it.[10]

Instead of bemoaning the fact that so many people are reading these stories or complaining that they denigrate or are opposed to the Christian message, we should be rejoicing that any literature causes such excitement. J. K. Rowling has a relationship with our children, and indeed with the child within us, which we should encourage. She is doing more for imagination than any other single force in our thoroughly bleak and businesslike century. The truth is that every one of us who has suffered through so-called 'free' education during the twentieth century is Harry Potter. Imagination was given no birthday party and had its room in a dust cupboard under the stairs.

---

[10] John Killinger, *God, The Devil, and Harry Potter* (New York: Thomas Dunne Books, 2002), p. 114.

Moses, Macbeth and Madame Montessori

We are all in the bowels of this giant machine, the modern global economy, being used as instruments to serve its ends. We have created this machine collectively, but we feel trapped individually. We've shifted the burden so much to the machine that we don't see a lot of options even though they may be really there. We can't go into the woods and live happily off the land anymore. So we 'deep freeze' our ability to sense what is actually going on. We deny the larger consequences of what we are doing.[11]

The problem of education has always been reduced to the analysis of three atomic elements that make up its constituent parts. These are the teacher, the pupil and the method whereby one exercises an influence over the other. Whether the educational system was 'teacher centred' or 'child centred', educational theory always took for granted the irreducible nature of the two focal points between which the more or less successful educational web was spun.

What we call the postmodern era has taken the rug from under this complacency. There are no fixed landmarks on the horizon. Before we establish the contours of either the teacher or the pupil we have to examine the educational situation. In terms of the philosophy of education, this means substituting a metaphysics of relationship for the age-old ontology of substance. In other words, the reality of the

---

[11] P. Senge, O. Scharmer, B. Flowers, J. Jaworski, *Presence: Exploring Profound Change in People, Organizations and Society* (New York: Doubleday, 2004), p. 232.

teacher and the pupil is derived from a more fundamental and all-embracing educational situation that gives meaning and significance to both.

But before introducing the new, let me outline the old. I have called the very ancient educational theory upon which most of our schooling is based the 'Moses, Macbeth and Madame Montessori syndrome'.[12] These three figures make up the chess pieces that are always constant factors in whatever game is played. The moves on the chessboard, no matter how complicated, are always some combination involving these three predetermined elements. Each one is separate and distinct and can be examined in its autonomous identity before any possible equation is proposed. The subject, whether pupil or teacher, is self-sufficient and self-contained. The pupil is really an underdeveloped version of the teacher. Both contain the possibility of grasping the universe surrounding them in an abstract and adult fashion within their own consciousness. The third term of this equation is dependent upon and derived from the definition of the other two: it is the method whereby the one causes the other to assume this identity.

I have chosen Moses to represent the first person of this educational trinity because he is a colourful and well-known example of the qualities and characteristics best suited to those engaged in the task of leading people to promised lands. The teacher, as primary substance in the educational equation, was seen as a strong, austere figure, called to lead the children out of the vague fog of primitive ignorance into the clear light of rational thinking.

Macbeth has been used to personify the pupil as the second term in the traditional equation. He has been chosen

---

[12] I developed this in *Phenomenology and Education*, Ph.D. thesis (National University of Ireland, 1976) and also in 'Education Since the Phenomenological Revolution', *The Black Book: An Analysis of Third Level Education*, Richard Kearney and Barré FitzPatrick, eds. (Dublin: Denham Press, 1975), pp. 70–83.

for his well-known association with evil on the one hand and his wavering indecision on the other. The reluctance of the normal child to insert themselves into the straitjacket deemed necessary for abstract omniscience, and the inevitable corollary that he murder all other pretenders to that throne make him a worthy patron. 'The voice of my education', to borrow a phrase from D. H. Lawrence, seems always to be asking me to kill it, my snake. And how like the voice of Lady Macbeth it sounds and has sounded as it echoes through the ages:

> Hie thee hither,
> That I may pour my spirits in thine ear;
> And chastise with the valour of my tongue
> All that impedes thee from the golden round,
> Which fate and metaphysical aid doth seem
> To have thee crown'd withal.[13]

Fate and the metaphysical aid of Western philosophy would seem to have destined Macbeth to the golden round, to that tiny circle of scientific consciousness where he is master, in an abstract and universal way, of all he surveys, and for which he must sacrifice all other possibilities. It was not always easy to achieve such anaesthesia. Some of the patients were even less willing to kill the snake or even scotch it than our venerable patron. That these two mascots are men is another hallmark and indictment of the Western European tradition we are outlining.

The third piece on the board is Madame Montessori. She has been chosen because her name has become identified with the idea of educational method. She represents the space between the two other pieces. It matters little whether she assumes the features of a tyrant or a seductress, her position of inferiority to the other two and her role as midwife to adulthood and abstraction have rarely been

---

[13] William Shakespeare, *Macbeth*, Act I, Scene 5, 27–31.

questioned. She has always derived her shape, form and texture in the Western tradition from whatever space remained after the other two contours had been sketched.

I have used this caricature to emphasise a basic structural truth, which could otherwise be lost in a mist of less significant detail. This truth is that the physiognomy of educational theory and practice, when reduced to an X-ray of its bone structure, has always maintained the same essential traits. No matter how subtle or varied a pattern has been woven around this simple structure, the three axiomatic and pivotal points remain constant.

It is true that changes have taken place in education at both the practical and the theoretical level, making it seem as if something has happened which revolutionised what went before; but these changes represent no more than reorganisation of the same paradigm. What we need if we wish to achieve the essential aim of education in the first place, is not just further and more refined manipulation of the pieces along the same lines, following the same rules and using the same board, but rather a complete upset of the board itself and the invention of a new game with redefinition of the pieces involved.

But you may ask, where does this description of 'all' education in the 'Western Tradition' come from? Is it not a fantastic caricature based on no factual evidence? To what does it apply? Are we supposed to accept that this glib description fits every school in every country in the West during the last how many centuries? And, even if we were to accept that the 'Moses, Macbeth and Madame Montessori' syndrome did hypnotise our educational thinking during this time, are we then to suppose that it had sufficient strength to effectively influence the whole of our civilisation up to the present day? Surely this places far too much emphasis on the scope of education, which until very recently affected only a minority of our population? Should we not accept, like Lady Bracknell, that 'fortunately in England, at any rate, education produces no effect whatsoever'.[14] Surely this apocalyptic denunciation does education far too much honour by declaring it guilty of crimes it has never had the energy or the influence to commit?

To the question 'how far back does this global condemnation actually stretch?' the answer would be 'as far back as could possibly matter to us in the present context'. An authentic relationship with our world has been replaced by a spurious one and this fallacy has been promoted and perpetrated, directly or indirectly, by education. The fact that education may never have been very widespread or effective does nothing to prevent it from exercising this extended influence. Education does not have to reach the core of every citizen in the universe to indoctrinate the world. On the contrary, the sin of education has been one of omission: it has failed to open our eyes to reality. It has rather endorsed the 'natural' view of the universe. Ever since the Greeks formulated this view in a coherent philosophy, the 'natural' tendency of civilisation was to accept this perfectly 'natural' viewpoint. It would have required an enormous educational effort to stimulate widespread and enduring rejection of this 'worldview' so solidly constructed and supported.

Ironically it was not the failure of this 'natural' thinking that brought about its replacement. It was, rather, its unprecedented success. Scientific positivism declared that there was nothing other than the real observable world and that we contained within ourselves the power to explain and to dominate this palpable reality. From this final triumph of reason we had reached our maturity. It had been necessary to pass from a mythological stage through a metaphysical stage to this ultimate and positive stage. For the intelligent adult, reason was lord. Nothing in reality could escape the penetration of logic. All could be reduced to principles, causes, reasons. Any other interpretations represented an infantile stage of humanity on its way towards the discovery

---

[14] Oscar Wilde, *The Importance of Being Earnest*, First Act.

of itself as sole interpreter of reality. This triumph of rationalism was paralleled in education by theories outlined by John Dewey:

> The subject matter of education consists of bodies of information and of skills that have been worked out in the past; therefore the chief business of the school is to transmit them to the new generation ... The main purpose or objective is to prepare the young for future responsibilities and for success in life, by means of acquisition of the organised bodies of information and prepared forms of skill which comprehend the material of instruction. Since the subject-matter as well as the standards of proper conduct are handed down from the past, the attitude of the pupils must, on the whole, be one of docility, receptivity and obedience ... teachers are the agents through which knowledge and skills are communicated and rules of conduct enforced.[15]

This view was reiterated by Schumacher in his influential book *Small is Beautiful*, in which he suggests that 'if Western civilisation is in a state of permanent crisis, it is not far-fetched to suggest that there may be something wrong with its education'. No civilisation has ever devoted more energy or resources to organised education than ours has, and the point of it all seems to be to train politicians, administrators and the entire community to know enough science so they can understand something of what the scientists are getting at. That we might at least be educated enough to know what scientists mean when they talk about the Second Law of Thermodynamics.[16]

---

[15] John Dewey, *Experience and Education* (New York: Collier, 1971), pp. 17–20.
[16] E. F. Schumacher, *Small is Beautiful* (London: Abacus edition, Sphere Books, 1974), pp. 64–6.

All of which shows that the main trends in 'traditional' education tend to place emphasis on the teacher as the proactive agent in the educational equation. The pupil is viewed as a passive receptacle and the middle term, the 'method', as a funnel which provides a one-way traffic system between the two. If we can accept this structural description of a certain dominant trend in educational theory and practice for the last few hundred years, then it is easier to describe more recent innovations in terms of opposition to this paradigm. The rise of so-called 'progressive' schools was the result of discontent with 'traditional' education and the two trends carried out a battle royal during the second half of the last century. Dewey summarises the quarrel as follows: 'The traditional scheme is, in essence, one of imposition from above and outside. It imposes adult standards, subject-matter and methods upon those who are only growing slowly towards maturity.' The gap is so great, he contends, that the subject matter, the methods of learning and behaving are foreign to the existing capacities of the young and are beyond their experience. This means that they have to be imposed, and although there are teachers who can devise methods to sugar-coat the pill, it is forced feeding. Education is 'to a large extent the cultural product of societies that assumed the future would be much like the past'.[17]

Dewey again summarises the philosophy of 'progressive' education: 'To imposition from above is opposed expression and cultivation of individuality; to external discipline is opposed free activity; to learning from texts and teachers, learning through experience.' He observes that these general principles do not solve any of the problems of management or practical running of such schools; they simply set out new problems which have to be solved on the basis of some philosophy of experience.

The question of whether Dewey himself was an educational philosopher of 'progressivism' is debateable and should not

---

[17] Ibid., pp. 18–19.

concern us here. The point is that education, especially on these islands, swerved and swayed between these two philosophies during the second half of the twentieth century. *The Black Papers* in Britain were a trenchant and articulate defence of the traditional approach to education.[18] The first one (1969) examined the 'Roots of the Trouble' and stated unequivocally that 'disastrous mistakes are being made in modern education, and that an urgent reappraisal is required of the assumptions on which "progressive" ideas, now in the ascendant, are based'.[19] Some years later the fifth *Black Paper* triumphantly declared that the 1960s were 'a disastrous period for the Western world, in which ill-thought-out notions of spontaneity, self-realisation and equality' invaded education. That 'hideous decade' gave way to the 1970s, which they hoped would witness 'a slow return to common sense'.[20] It is of interest to note, in this context, that the reform of the Irish Primary School Curriculum dates from 1971. G. H. Bancock, in an article entitled 'Progressivism and the Content of Education' in that same *Black Paper* of 1975, describes the difference between traditional and progressive education as a shift in our metaphysical image of ourselves 'from a self that has to be made to a self that simply has to be expressed'.[21] The defenders of this traditionalist philosophy of education refuse to imagine the possibility that something revolutionary may have occurred within the very framework of that 'European culture' which they are so anxious to preserve. The 'progressives' are asking for a more comprehensive view of what knowing is all about, what being human is all about, and what education is all about.

---

[18] Mark Patrick Hederman, 'The Black Papers and Education in the Eighties', *Educational Theory in a Changing World, Journal of the Institute of Education*, V. A. McClelland, ed., University of Hull (Jubilee Number, 1980), pp. 23–31.
[19] *Black Paper One: Fight for Education*, C. B. Cox and A. E. Dyson, eds., London, 1969.
[20] *Black Paper 1977*, C. B. Cox and Rhodes Boyson, eds., p. 13.
[21] *Black Paper 1975*, C. B. Cox and Rhodes Boyson, eds., p. 20.

However, it seems to me that both these trends, identified in a caricature as 'traditional' and 'progressive', remain within the Moses, Macbeth and Madame Montessori framework. The first emphasises Moses as the main part in the play, whereas the second puts the emphasis on Macbeth. It seems to me that the educational equation cannot be approached in terms of two distinct and separately analysable subjects, a teacher and a child, but as a situation within which these two elements comprise an essential and inseparable unit. There is no such thing as a teacher or a pupil as realities in themselves. The two, even as words, are defined in terms of their relationship and can only be analysed within the context of the educational encounter. There is no such thing as an independent and autonomous entity definable in terms of itself and then placed 'in' an educational situation as two marbles might be placed upon a cushion. The teacher and the pupil are already in contact with one another as beings-in-the-world. There are lifelines that stretch through them and destroy any myth of their perfect autonomy. These underground tendrils have to be detected and unveiled before the true reality of either of them can be enunciated. We have to recognise that subjectivity is not a self-contained unit, that the teacher and the pupil are not sealed and separated into their own particular identities; they are stretched way beyond themselves through a plethora of intentional roots which connect them to each other and to the world in which they live and have their being.

The subject, closed in on itself, which was once the metaphysical source of both self and the world, has been shown up as an invention, an abstraction, a translation made by us. The postmodern world, as it is called, provides us with a new concept of knowing. It refuses to restrict 'knowledge' to particular faculties or limited zones of consciousness within the human organism, as though knowledge were an almost accidental quality superimposed upon, or grafted into, an alien substance. Instead, it redistributes 'knowledge' throughout the whole human structure like some all-pervasive liquid which would seep into every pore of the organism and, like yeast in bread, would leaven the whole batch. Knowing is the activity of me alive in the body. Human acts do not have to accede to some threshold of scientific rationality before they can qualify as 'thought'. Thinking is our way of existing: the body is a pulsating sponge of knowing contact with the world. There is no part of me, or moment of my life, that ever ceases to perform the knowing function. Thinking, as my way of existing, assumes every contour and invades every particle of myself.[22] In this way knowledge becomes identified with the existence of the being so endowed, which has at least two serious repercussions. The first is at the level of

---

[22] As an example of such philosophy I quote Maurice Merleau-Ponty, *The Structure of Behaviour* (London: Methuen, 1965), p. 172: 'The conception of consciousness which we must formulate is profoundly modified. It is no longer possible to define it as a universal function for the organisation of experience which would impose on all its objects the conditions of logical and physical existence which are those of a universe of articulated objects and which would owe its specifications only to the variety of its contents. There will be sectors of experience that are irreducible to each other. At the same time that one abandons the notion of the "multiple given" as the source of all specifications, one will doubtless be obliged to abandon the notion of mental activity as the principle of all co-ordinations. Indeed, as soon as one refuses to separate the relation from the different concrete structures which appear in experience, it is no longer possible to found all relation on the activity of the "epistemological subject"; and, at the same time as the perceived world is fragmented into discontinuous "regions", consciousness is divided into different types of acts of consciousness. In particular, the fact that primitive perception is, as it were, haunted by human presence and lacunary for all the rest obliges us to accept the fact that "others", although they may be reached in adults through "sensations" or "images", can also be known by means of very impoverished representational contents. Therefore, there must be several ways for consciousness to intend its object and several sorts of intentions in it. To possess and contemplate a "representation" and to co-ordinate a mosaic of sensations are special attitudes which cannot account for all the life of consciousness and which probably apply to its more primitive modes, as a translation applies to a "text".'

knowledge as epistemology. Knowledge can no longer be identified with, or measured and transmitted as a series of ououoicoe or facts designed to feed one particular area of human intelligence. The notion of 'a knowledgeable person' becomes a tautology. A person is more or less 'knowledgeable' to the extent that he or she is more or less a person. Education ceases to be the promotion of certain specialised faculties and the distribution of facts. It becomes the promotion of the person as a totality designed to make personal contact with the surrounding world.

The second is at the level of knowledge as pedagogy. There can be no knowledge which does not begin by sparking off real contact between the human organism and its world. Unless some interior pulse is touched into movement from a personal source that recognises itself as such, no knowledge and no education has yet begun. It is possible to inject facts into an amorphous container but this only serves to prolong a sleep of paralysis and preserve an illusion of progress. The task is therefore to reconstruct an educational apparatus that can cater for this newly discovered situation. All future educational endeavours must begin with analysis of its most fundamental datum – the pedagogical encounter, the educational relationship – which becomes the first term and the regulating norm of the investigation. Teacher and pupil must be redefined, not in isolation, but in terms of the specific relationship demanded of them by the educational situation. This means that the learning process must begin with an awareness of a personal centre of significant living. From such a place all experience becomes meaningful: 'Learning is not the accumulation of scraps of knowledge; it is a growth, wherein every act of knowledge develops the subject, thus making it capable of constituting ever more and more complex objectivities – and the objective growth in complexity parallels the subjective growth in capacity.'[23] The

---

[23] Quentin Lauer, *Phenomenology: Its Genesis and Prospect* (New York: Harper Torchbooks, 1965), p. 105.

movement would describe an ever-widening sweep of a pendulum increasing the sensitivity of the person and developing the width, depth and splendour of the circumambient world.

Education must cease to be either the filtering of facts into dull or bright receptacles, or the anarchical exacerbation of any and every unbridled instinct. It must spark the organismic throb which constitutes the knowing humanity of every child and then guide and direct this in whatever direction is necessary to allow each of these potential centres of meaning to stretch fully across the reality of the universe.

To say that something can be known is not to say that anyone can know it. A child has certain experiences which allow it to know certain things and make it capable of knowing. But 'it is capable only of such knowledge as the stream of its previous experience warrants'.[24] Knowledge is not fundamentally a technique or a craft, it is a way of being, of being myself. So let us try to leave this squabbling trio behind and enter the brave new world of the twenty-first century, the world of text and tweet.

---

[24] Ibid., p. 104.

CHAPTER THREE

Imagination in Education

Every child is an artist. The problem is how to remain an artist once we grow up.

Pablo Picasso

In Ireland we seem to have arrived at a compromise solution which is now beginning to show some incompatibilities. The reforms of the Irish primary school curriculum in 1971 introduced a 'child-centred' ethos that many have welcomed but that some have accused of being over-influenced by 'progressive' tendencies. On the other hand, the Leaving Certificate requirements of our secondary school curriculum rely heavily on the more traditional philosophy of education. The question we are now being asked, by those who have analysed the results of over forty years of the new curriculum in our primary schools, is this: have the excesses of 'progressivism' made inroads upon the daily conduct of primary education in Ireland?

And the answer seems to be 'yes' if we are to take Literacy and Numeracy for Learning and Life: The National Strategy to Improve Literacy and Numeracy among Children and Young People (July 2011), at its face value. If the new curriculum had been working properly there would have been no need to launch these strategies for running repairs. So, the primary school curriculum is working off one set of educational principles and the secondary schools find these wanting because they fail to produce in our school-going population the skills necessary to cope with entry requirements to third-level education. The battleground now becomes the Junior Certificate examination. Is this to be the crowning vindication of all the child-centred creativity espoused by our enlightened curriculum in primary schools? Or is it to be a no-nonsense attempt to redress the balance and knock our school-going population into shape for the real world of Leaving Certificate points? At present, most of the literature available seems to point towards the latter conclusion. And this, to my mind, is a mistake.

Sixty thousand people in Ireland every year, who want to get adequate points in their final examinations, have to give up the last two years of school life to filling their heads with irrelevant knowledge, which they then have to regurgitate in long hand on a particular day at the start of the summer. Our whole examination system at this level is out of date, and is based on a completely different culture from the one that now swamps us all. And the sad truth is that we all know this but we cannot face the task of replacing it.

On Monday, 16 August 2010, publication of research documentation by the Economic and Social Research Institute (ERSI) showed clearly that the punishing study regimes we are imposing on our children, especially as they are leaving secondary school, are affecting their health, their welfare and their personal development. Not only is this an established fact, these regimes are failing to equip students for the second decade of the twenty-first century. Two years later nothing has been done to show that we have understood these findings.

Many were outraged because neither Seamus Heaney nor Sylvia Plath appeared on the Higher Level paper for honours English in the Leaving Certificate this year. Both had been predicted and Paddy Power had given serious odds on their appearance. No one knows exactly how Plath and Heaney gained their status as 'The Poets Who Will Come Up This Year'. In the game of Leaving Cert roulette, students are advised to be familiar with five of eight poets on the course. However, by a process of elimination (Who came up last year? Is there a female poet? Or an Irish one?), students cut this number down to one or two favourites. The job of most English teachers is to make such predictions accurately. You're a 'great teacher' if you guess correctly; you're a dud if you don't. What this tells us about the teaching of poetry in our schools is pathetic. What it tells us about the whole Leaving Certificate system should be decisive. But it is not. The *Irish Times* editorial on the day the Leaving Cert began this year spelt out the facts: 'The Leaving Cert remains a high-stakes exam because of its role as the main gateway to higher education. Minister for Education, Ruairí Quinn, has been openly critical of the Leaving Cert because of its old-fashioned stress on rote learning and its heavy reliance on one terminal exam.' But the minister doesn't intend to do anything about it until 2022, even though 'University presidents, employers and educationalists have all joined in the chorus of criticism.' There's an increasing sense that the Leaving Cert is cut adrift from the needs of the Irish economy. 'Employers complain how they find it difficult to source multilingual, tech-savvy students even with the current levels of unemployment. University heads say many Leaving Cert students – even those with strong grades – are unable to cope with the independent learning expected of them at third level.'[25]

Many parents and teachers worry that the exam fails to fire a genuine love of literature or any area of study. Most students never want to see a Shakespeare play again after they have been through the torture of shredding one for their final exam. The only poem many of them 'love' is the one correctly forecast by their teacher, which they learnt off the notes for, giving them the grades needed to go where they want at third level. The consequences in this third level pastureland were spelt out by Dr Greg Foley of Dublin City University in a letter to the *Irish Times* two days after the article cited above.

---

[25] *Irish Times* (16 June 2012).

So while the Leaving Certificate is not providing us in the sector with well-prepared students, we are clearly failing to fix whatever deficiencies they might have. Indeed rather than fixing the problem, we are merely perpetuating the problems of the second-level system by increasingly 'coaching' our students through their studies. In a way, we have no alternative unless we are willing to accept massive attrition rates – and the expected political fallout ... Ultimately, we get a third-level sector that increasingly has to adopt second-level methods to drag academically weak students through the system.[26]

Ruairí Quinn has recently published the view that 'it is generally felt that the Leaving Certificate curriculum is satisfactory, but that it has been captured by a number of demands and requirements'. He lists these as the points race for entry to university and the 'high degree of predictability' that 'leads to a focus of teaching to the test rather than covering the syllabus in its entirety' and 'the proliferation of undergraduate courses and options which are designed ... to attract high-points-achieving students'.[27] Such an attempt to validate the examination in itself by attributing its shortcomings to outside influences is hardly likely to convince the many teachers, parents, employers and students who know that the Leaving Certificate itself, as a regurgitation on one single day of the year of material learned off by heart, which is of little use to those required to memorise, is an out-of-date exercise as ineffective as it is counter-productive. The entire educational process, in effect, was designed with the aim of maximising the number of points racked up as its number one priority. When you talk to teachers, they complain bitterly too. They know that their

---

[26] Dr Greg Foley in a letter to the *Irish Times* (8 June 2012).
[27] Ruairí Quinn, 'The Future Development of Education in Ireland', *Studies* 101.402 (Summer 2012), pp. 130–1.

job should be about more than simply preparing pupils to get through an exam in the most efficient manner possible. But they also know that if they didn't put exam results at the top of the agenda, then the parents, the school and even, in some cases, the students themselves, would resent it.

So, why do we not set about replacing it immediately? The only person who can take such decisive action is Ruairí Quinn, the Minister for Education, who refuses to act. We can't do anything about it at present, he claims, because reform of the Leaving Cert must await his ongoing Junior Cert reform package, due to be rolled out from 2017. It seems extraordinary, the editorial in the *Irish Times* continues, that

> the education system is continuing with an exam widely regarded as being well past its 'sell-by' date. The delay is all the more shocking, given that a template for a more modern exam is already in place. The National Council for Curriculum and Assessment has been developing a range of proposals for various education ministers since 2006. At this stage, it's clear the new exam should place a new stress on self-directed, independent learning and critical thinking.

Do we continue to have an anachronistic and nostalgic sense of pride in our education system dating back to the days when the IDA held us up as a model for multinationals to locate here and use our skilled workforce? Things have changed, we have not. We are still working the out-of-date, early-twentieth-century model which saw schools as assembly lines to provide children with chunks of knowledge necessary to work in a relatively rigid hierarchical society where memory and obeying rules were all you needed to be an efficient and obedient cog in the wheel. Where the school year was broken up according to the farming cycles and the necessity of having help at home with the harvest. Half of our children's abilities lie latent in this memory-based race for points. And now college, or university, has become like secondary school, with students demanding notes for what will come up in exams so that they can learn everything off by heart. Who needs to memorise vast chunks of information when we have Google? And what kind of job based on the obedient following of rules has not been computerised or designed for robots? The whole obsolete factory model of education has to be challenged and replaced. Why should we all be educated in our age groups, as if from our date of manufacture? Many children are better than others at some subjects. Why should we impose this standardisation – why do you have to do everything together because you are the same age? We have to change our paradigm and our production-line mentality.

The education system currently in place in Ireland is potentially a weapon of mass destruction where imagination is concerned. An education based upon memory presumes that the past is normative and that the future will be more of the same. We must know by now that the future, even ten years down the line, may be so different from the world we now experience that our parents will find themselves quite disoriented. We will find that we have trained our children in the wrong direction. We concentrated on memory where we should have been honing their imaginative skills. We should have been preparing them for a world beyond anything we had ever dreamed possible.

Even our universities, where critical and imaginative thinking should be fostered, seem to have, in some cases, sold the pass. Research projects financed by multinationals, sometimes housed on the campus, often call the shots. The places where our future should be sketched out in broad and imaginative sketches have become bastions of business where the present can be shored up and consolidated.

We should not harness our children to the business needs or the short-term economic growth of this country. Just because a multinational company is offering payment for a number of jobs to be done, does not mean that our children's prospects should be tailored to meet this requirement. A new form of slavery to the imperative of economic growth should not become the aim of our educational system. Instead of making our educational system fit the targets of some economic plan in terms of market needs and jobs on offer, we should be listening to the voices of the children. These are the prophetic voices of the future.

We are told that science will save us. It won't. It will help, of course, and has performed miracles in our world, but it is not everything. We need thinking outside the box. We need imagination to sketch the future. There must be a privileged place for imagination and the arts in our education system:

> I believe that the arts lie dreaming of things to come ... Its importance is greater because it comes to us at the moment when we are beginning to be interested in many things which positive science, the interpreter of exterior law, has always denied: communion of mind with mind in thought and without words, foreknowledge in dreams and in visions, and the coming among us of the dead, and of much else. We are, it may be, at a crowning crisis of the world, at the moment when man is about to ascend, with the wealth he has been so long gathering upon his shoulders, the stairway he has been descending from the first days ... The arts are, I believe, about to take on their shoulders the burdens that have fallen from the shoulders of priests, and to lead us back upon our journey by filling our thoughts with the essences of things, and not with things.[28]

---

[28] W. B. Yeats, 'The Autumn of the Body' (1898), *Essays & Introductions* (London: MacMillan, 1961), p. 193.

We have borrowed our education systems from armies, conquerors, mathematicians, scientists, technologists. These should provide only one half of what education might mean, if even that. The industrial revolution, the scientific revolution, the technological revolution, the cybernetic revolution: all these have transformed our lives and we are grateful to them. We know also that they need young hands to keep them going, to make them work, to maintain the infrastructure of our Western world. But these very important realities with which our education system is obsessed have been allowed to crowd out the tiny flowers of imagination. There must be more to life than science; there is more to science than technology. That more is an inner garden of the imagination which each of us should be allowed to cultivate, where we should be encouraged to dwell for at least some part of our days and lives. Our children have no time for dilly-dallying, no space for inner or outer exploration, no opportunity for dreaming. Every minute of every day is full up with 'learning'. They have to get through the 'core subjects' of the curriculum, they have to do their 'homework', they have to practice cramming, they have to do their examinations, they have to aim for the points awarded for these examinations – they have no time to be children, they've grown up before they were allowed to know what was happening.

Education should be child-centred. Again we hear this cliché mouthed everywhere and we read it in every education document ever written. But as it is, in Ireland at any rate, the child is the very last item in the pecking order. We are overloaded with bureaucracy: government ministers, departments of education and teachers' trade unions fill up three quarters of the picture. The amount of negativity around this narrative is numbing. When the adults have finished quarrelling and negotiating, we turn to the topic of what they are meant to be there for in the first place. In the meantime the children grow up, one year at a time, for every year the 'authorities' spend shoring up a model that is out of date, and producing finished products unable to cope with the complexities of the world they have inherited, and out of touch with the reality of who they are in themselves.

What should we do? Somehow we have to ambush the freight train and take back our education system to ourselves and for our children. We have all that we need to do this already within our grasp and the downturn in the economy is probably our greatest ally at this time. At least this downturn means that the government cannot buy the straitjackets for everyone they had been hoping to, and cannot provide enough chicken coops to make battery fowl out of all our fledglings.

The axe inevitably falls where the arts and creativity are involved. This has already happened where funding for in-service in terms of the arts has been reduced and where intervention is reserved for schools perceived as being backward. These are targeted by SWAT teams who will bring them up to standard, meaning the standard set by examination results and requirements for entry to third-level establishments.

So, fortunately, the model we have cannot be sustained and there is no chequebook solution to the future of education. In Ireland we have all the great teachers we need; there are hundreds being educated by our training colleges each year. All we have to do is show these young people how to release imagination and how to access creativity in themselves, so that they can allow these forces to spread throughout every educational establishment in the land.

You don't have to do anything very ambitious. Imagination is always and already huge in children, you only have to release it, encourage it, guide and direct it. And not too prescriptively either. Just let the flowers blossom of their own accord. Imagination, to borrow a phrase from Alan McGlashan, is 'a golden key that is the careless plaything of all children, and the conscious instrument of a few geniuses'.[29]

---

[29] Alan McGlashan, *Savage and Beautiful Country: The Secret Life of the Mind* (New York: Hillstone, 1966), p. 11.

Ireland's greatest asset is imagination. It seeps through every aspect of our cultural lives in spite of its neglect in our schools. How many poets, musicians, painters, rock stars, dancers, storytellers, entrepreneurs left school at fourteen, fifteen, sixteen, and began their real education the moment they stepped into the University of Life? Imagination is what we should be cherishing, encouraging, cultivating, instead of which we are systematically deleting it from the desktop of every child who wants to get enough points in the Leaving Certificate to enter our third-level institutes. The pressures from the system against growth to full potential are so great that drastic intervention is necessary to redress the balance. In fact, the new curriculum at primary level has improved immeasurably. However, the training of teachers to allow them to operate this new curriculum creatively is still deficient.

Creative teachers make creative classrooms, which, in turn, make for creative children. We do have an enviable success story to record in the area of creative writing: four Nobel laureates in one century, not to speak of the growing number of poets, dramatists, novelists and artists who show us evidence of genius every day. Our task as educators is to harness this natural flair, simply by allowing it some free play within our educational systems. This country should be and could be an incubator of the imagination, a role model for others. And the truth is that, as teachers, we don't have to do anything. Creativity is already there – as Picasso says: every child is a born artist. Although children innately engage in divergent thinking, Ken Robinson cites a study called *Breakpoint and Beyond*, which shows that our ability to think divergently dries up as we pass through the education system. At kindergarten level, 98 per cent of children are able to attain genius level. Retested at the age of 8–10, and then again at 13–15, this capacity has deteriorated dramatically. In school, divergent thinking is a fish out of water.[30]

---

[30] George T. Ainsworth-Land and Beth Jarman, *Breakpoint and Beyond: Mastering the Future Today* (New York: HarperBusiness, 1992).

Lynne had been underperforming at school, so her mother took her to the doctor and explained about her never being able to sit down in the classroom for one moment in one place. She was always fidgeting and suffered from lack of focus. After hearing everything her mother said, the doctor told Lynne that he needed to talk to her mother privately for a moment. He turned on the radio and walked out of the room. He then encouraged the mother to look at Lynne, who was dancing to the radio. 'There's nothing wrong with your daughter,' the doctor said, 'except that she's a dancer and no one has encouraged her.' Gillian Barbara Lynne (born 20 February 1926) became a famous choreographer noted for *Cats* and the longest running musical on Broadway, *Phantom of the Opera*. How many 'mute inglorious Miltons' and listless unemployed Lynnes have been stifled by 'free' education? General Montgomery tells in his memoirs of a governess he had who used to say every morning: 'Go out and see what that child is doing and stop him.' Our education system has adopted a similar mantra.

From four years of age our children are treated to a bookish, commercial education. Recent meetings of the United Nations seem determined to inflict this myopia on all children of the world in the name of equality of opportunity and universal education. In Europe this plan manifested itself in the Lisbon agreement implemented in December 2009.

When the European Council met in Lisbon, Portugal, in March 2000, EU leaders adopted a ten-year programme aimed at revitalising growth and sustainable development across the EU. They noted the challenges Europe was facing from globalisation, an ageing population, and the emergence of a worldwide information society. They resolved that economic and social reforms had to take place in the context of 'a positive strategy which combines competitiveness and social cohesion', and reaffirmed that the European social model, with its developed systems of social protection, must underpin the strategy. The Union 'set itself a new strategic goal for the next decade: to become the most competitive and dynamic knowledge-based economy in the world, capable of sustainable economic growth with more and better jobs and greater social cohesion'.[31]

Is this the future we want for our children? Is this all that our education system should hold for them?

---

[31] European Council of Heads of State or Government (2000), p. 3.

CHAPTER FOUR

Education as Personal Relationship

> We dance round in a ring and suppose,
> But the Secret sits in the middle and knows.[32]

M artin Buber (1878–1965), the Jewish philosopher, burst onto the scene in 1923 with an essay on human existence called *Ich und Du*, later translated into English in 1936 as *I and Thou*. This influential work about the fundamental nature of our lives as dialogue spawned the philosophical school of Personalism and had repercussions on all twentieth-century movements of thought from existentialism to Vatican II. It also provides us with an original theory of education and one which undercuts the division we have been describing between traditionalist and progressive education and the Moses, Macbeth and Madame Montessori syndrome. The teacher is the midwife of genuine personhood. Buber's theory of education shifts the emphasis from the teacher and the pupil to the space between them. That space is the all-important one and is the most fundamental educational reality.

Education, in the end, means a certain kind of relationship between a teacher and a pupil. We see this writ large in the case of George VI of England and his speech therapist, Lionel Logue, portrayed in the film *The King's Speech*, which won so many Oscar awards in 2010. Here the new king is forced to find his own voice and is fortunate

---

[32] Robert Frost, 'The Secret Sits', *The Poetry of Robert Frost*, Edward Connery Lathem, ed. (New York: Henry Holt, 1979), p. 362.

enough to meet the person who can help him to achieve this goal. But it is not just royal personages who need such highly personal attention. From birth to adolescence, the human person, like plants in general, needs sheltered conditions and personal attention for maximum growth. Small is beautiful when it comes to schools. The secret of education is to have a better teacher–student ratio: this is more important than having expensive facilities and up-to-date equipment. Communication between people is vital for any form of education, as the essential element is person-to-person contact. Real education is a duet between the person of the teacher and the person of the student. Unless the life of dialogue can be inserted fully into educational practice, education ceases to be a fully human or humanising activity.

Geniuses don't need education from anyone – they flower in spite of circumstances. But geniuses are few, and the average child needs care and individual attention from competent and dedicated adults in a small environment to develop their own personalities. Unless such education is available to our children, then let's not pretend that what we are offering is 'education'. Instruction can take place in a warehouse; education is the miracle that happens between people who have the time and the imagination to engage at a personal level in the very precise and creative activity that is educational relationship. It is possible to impart instruction to any number of people, even by electronic means over great distances, but the secret of education is transmission from person to person. So, often, education is at present a matter of luck: meeting the right person at the right time. But such luck is more likely to happen in a small environment where real educational dialogue is possible.

There is a professional relationship between doctors and patients, analysts and analysands; there are codes of conduct, declarations and bills of human rights, governing human relationships in most situations of authority and control, and yet there was not any equivalent strategy in Ireland giving guidelines for educators and teachers until the beginning of this century.[33] When I began teaching at the end of the 1960s I became aware of the need for such standards and so I decided to try to work these out for myself before I engaged in teaching professionally. I spent some years doing a doctorate on the specific kind of relationship that should exist between a teacher and a pupil. At the end of this, I became convinced that education is essentially a relationship such as Martin Buber describes, and education cannot be reality for most children unless they are beneficiaries of this sort of educational contact.

Each one of us has a social orbit around us, something like an aura or an atmosphere, which is the invisible extension of ourselves. You might call it potential space. There used to be an ad on TV showing children who had eaten Ready Brek in the morning. These children were surrounded by a warm, enveloping rainbow with the slogan 'Get up and Glow'. They had a radiant space around them, ready to meet anything or anyone. This advertisement gives an idea of the kind of potential space surrounding each one of us as individuals and into which we have to expand if we are to develop as persons. We are born individuals and we become persons by moving into this space between us and other persons. Some of us never manage to expand into this space and therefore never appropriate it. It remains uninhabited. Such people never really move comfortably

---

[33] The Teaching Council of Ireland published in June of this year, 2012, a new Code of Professional Conduct for Teachers which sets out the standards of professional knowledge, skill, competence and conduct expected. They list thirty-three such standards that reflect the complexity and variety of teaching and cover areas such as communication and relationships, equality and inclusion, compliance with national and school policies, professional development and student welfare. The standards are underpinned by four core values: respect, care, integrity and trust.

into the realm of sociability. They remain individuals. The great enemy to such stretching out into our circumjacent ring of confidence is fear. Even physiologically, the manifestations of fear are a moving away from this outer periphery. We go white, as they say, or we faint; but really what happens is that our energy and our bodily fluids retreat from the surface of our skin and drain back towards the centre. The opposite occurs when we meet someone we really like. Everything in us moves out towards that person and the blood rushes, as they say, to our cheeks. What I am suggesting is that beyond even that skin which has been suffused with 'a glow', there is a space which surrounds each one of us, and the most important goal of education is to allow each child to inhabit that space so that he or she may cease to be an individual wrapped up in their own cocoon but may develop into a full person, open to and expanding into that space between us and other people. We are born individuals but we become persons by appropriating and inhabiting this space.

D. W. Winnicott, in his lifelong study of child psychiatry, has shown that, as well as the physical substance that is every child's reality as a body, there is another no less real part of ourselves, which he calls 'potential space'.[34] This relational orbit is neither entirely interior nor entirely exterior. It has to be appropriated and expanded into by each of us, which is not possible unless the child is coaxed into it by a contagious atmosphere of trust. Unless the child can relax and be confirmed by the surrounding environment, it will retire within the confines of the substantial bodily self and the potential space will eventually evaporate. The removal of this dimension not only limits the expansive growth of the child, it also has a detrimental effect on the cauterised remains. The child has to organise its substantial self not in terms of welcoming and out-going

---

[34] D. W. Winnicott, *The Child, The Family, and the Outside World* and *Playing and Reality* (London: Penguin, 1971).

transitivity, but in the grip of frightened and hostile defensiveness. It is rather like a snail cautiously unfurling itself into the sunshine of the outside world. If you pour acid on it just as it comes out, it will retreat as hastily as it can and never again take the risk of venturing forth. The educator's role is to establish with the pupil that specific contact which will unlock the armour and allow the person to expand. This contact is the primary word in education. It establishes a trust: 'Trust, trust in the world, because this human being exists – that is the most inward achievement of the relation in education.'[35]

There are other relationships making up the web of successful education. Relationship with God, relationship with family, relationship with peers. But the relationship with the teacher is paramount. It is a contact rather than a content. Unless teachers are aware of and trained towards this delicate weave, this ultimate responsibility, it can go very wrong. But contact there must be. For there has to be an electricity in the air. If not, there is no ether on which the educational relationship can travel. But unless you have dealt with this reality in yourself, this exciting capacity for exhilarating contact, unless it has been sealed with the breath of the Holy Spirit, it can be harmful.

The most important question for every teacher is 'Why do I teach? What motivation inspires me to do so?' The being of every teacher is defined by this motivation or will to teach. Without it there is no teaching at all. The analysis and examination of the kind of motivation is another thing, a second step. The first step is to be aware that some will to teach is a prerequisite, without which no one should embark upon this activity. One often hears the praises sung of the 'dedicated' teacher who is 'completely detached'. The idea would seem to be that the 'virtuous' teacher is one who finds no pleasure, no fulfilment in this work other than the

---

[35] Martin Buber, *Between Man and Man* (New York: Macmillan, 1964), p. 125.

routine daily sacrifice to duty. The teacher who clocks in every morning in answer to the call of duty to inform these faceless numbers, is regarded by some as the model for all who undertake such work.

Without some motivation or interest no one can teach. Education without contact is impotent. This option for 'contact' as the primary word of education opposes, for instance, the view that the teacher is not there for the student, or the student for the teacher, but that both are there for the sake of science. In this view, the educational relationship is a dispensable commodity. We could arrive at a stage where television could replace the teacher and tape recorders could act as successful substitute for the educational experience. Buber says in this context:

> If we ever reach the stage of making ourselves understood only by means of the dictograph, that is, without contact with one another, the chance of human growth would be indefinitely lost.[36]

Obviously, this notion does not exclude the necessity of formal teaching, organised curriculum and objective science. These make up an essential part of any serious educational programme. But, unless they are inserted into the framework of the educational relation, they never assume the reality of communion, and so they fail to promote the total growth of the student. All education, no matter how technical or scientific, must be pervaded by the dimension of dialogue. The question is this: are you capable of standing in direct relation? And in the area which concerns us here: what kind of person is capable of standing in that particular form of direct relation which is education?

---

[36] Buber, *The Knowledge of Man* (New York: Harper & Row, 1966), p. 67.

Although we may not be able to define exactly the laws of genuine educating, this does not mean that such activity remains an indescribable exercise of charismatic genius. It is not true that teachers are born and not made. It is possible to outline the structure and define the limits of this relation, and it is the duty of anyone assuming this task to articulate this knowledge which 'in no way resists personal comprehension and penetration'. Those who say that they haven't the time to theorise, that they have to get on with the job, would be well advised to consider what job they are getting on with. There is no such thing as a 'natural' teacher. The educator must, and can, be trained.

The fact that we can make contact with children, that we have 'a way of getting on with them', is not enough. We have to carefully examine this 'way' and purify this 'contact' before we can call it education. It is not enough to mean well. The will to educate is not sufficient in itself. It has to be purified of 'self-will' and become 'the will to educate'. Buber states quite bluntly, even harshly, that 'one only needs to read, say, the accounts of Pestalozzi's teaching method to see how easily, even with the noblest teachers, arbitrary self-will is mixed up with will'.[37] It is necessary to know ourselves and to know what we should be trying to do. Armed with this double knowledge we should be able to achieve that unity of will and purpose that will allow us to fulfil this task.

This leads us to an essential paradox. Education is said to be the fully spontaneous presence of the being of the teacher, and, at the same time, it requires of the teacher a careful critical analysis and submission to 'the structure of proportions and the limits' of its 'special objectivity'. Unless we are prepared to unravel the subtle knot of such 'paradoxical legitimacy' with a great deal of patience, we cannot hope to understand the fragile reality Buber proposes. On the one hand Buber says:

---

[37] Buber, *Between Man and Man*, p. 127.

> Only in his whole being, in his spontaneity can the educator truly affect the whole being of his pupil. For educating characters you do not need a moral genius, but you do need a man who is wholly alive and able to communicate himself to his fellow men.[38]

And on the other hand Buber is very severe in his condemnation of naïve enthusiasm and unscientific good will. How is it possible to be spontaneous and reflective at the same time?

The answer is that this spontaneity is not just something natural or effortless. It is the result of a remarkable human achievement which allows us to act directly from the fullness of our being. This 'unity of being' has to be accomplished before undertaking any great work, and only those who have done so are qualified to teach.[39] The teacher must be the 'spiritual' person, which means that they must have achieved unity of spirit. This does not mean the dominance of any one faculty over others but 'the unity of all faculties within the personality'. This is what constitutes our 'wholeness' and it is this that Buber calls 'spirit'. Once this has been achieved it gives a new and 'spontaneous' life to the 'spiritual' person. It is a struggle that gradually forms a habit within us:

> Thus man ultimately reaches a point where he can rely upon his soul, because its unity is so great that it overcomes contradiction with effortless ease. In place of all his former great efforts all that is now necessary is a relaxed vigilance.[40]

---

[38] Ibid., p. 134.

[39] Buber, *Pointing the Way: Collected Essays* (New York: Humanity Books, 1999), p. 105.

[40] Maurice Friedman, *Martin Buber: The Life of Dialogue* (London: Routledge, 2002), p. 68.

This new unity, from which the natural spontaneity of the person of the spirit flows, is a point reached after a long struggle which explains the apparent paradox between spontaneity and the learned response. Buber refers to the 'spiritual' in the next quotation as something which supplements the wherewithal of the natural person:

> In education there is a lofty asceticism: an asceticism which rejoices in the world, for the sake of the responsibility for a realm of life which is entrusted to us for our influence but not for our interference – either by the will to power or by Eros ... Giving and withholding oneself, intimacy and distance, which of course must not be controlled by reflection, but must arise from the living tact of the natural and spiritual man.[41]

Those who wish to educate must, first of all, be aware of the precise realm of being for which they are responsible and then must achieve in themselves that unity of purpose and desire which will supply them with a 'natural' capacity to respond to this vocation. This will come first of all by reflection, but must flower into effortless ease if it is to be effective. Spirit is our totality become conscious, the totality which both comprises and integrates all our capacities, powers, qualities and urges. Spiritual life is nothing but our existence insofar as we possess this 'true human conscious totality'.

The educator must become such to the very core of their being, possessed by them in full consciousness of the totality of their situation. And it is not enough to have achieved our own unity of being. As teachers, we must, first of all, have the capacity to recognise the 'reality' of the particular person confronting us. This realism is essential to our task. But it is not enough. We must also have the

---

[41] Buber, *Between Man and Man*, p. 122.

imaginative flair that allows us to divine the possibilities
potentially present in every pupil and the secret which will
release these. Such a combination of realism and
imagination is the specific flair of the educator.

This flair is given a special name by Buber, which
combines both its elements. He calls it *Realphantasie* in
German. It means that whatever is lacking from the pupil's
side has to be supplemented by the teacher. 'Realistic
imagination' allows the teacher to work the relationship
from the pupil's side also, as though they were a paralysed
limb that had to be supported, until the strength of the
relation grows to maturity and the teacher can withdraw this
educative subvention. This 'supreme artistry of the teacher'
sees the full being of the child, recognises what stands
between the child and such fullness, and knows the secret
of how to remove these obstacles. A genuine teacher has to
be motivated by the one desire to release real being in the
child without seeking to enjoy it or appropriate it.

More than that we must cultivate that 'realistic
imagination' which allows the other to be as they are,
because each person must achieve unity of being in their
own way. Here is what Buber means by the 'realistic
imagination' which creates the paradoxical legitimacy of an
influence which is, on the one hand, 'direct relation' and, on
the other, appropriate to the situation of the pupil:

> 'Realistic imagination ... is the capacity of putting
> before the soul a reality which exists in the present
> moment but which cannot be perceived through the
> senses.' This is particularly valid about the reality of
> other people. The person who is educated to a
> realistic imagination will observe the other as he is.
> This contrasts to the artistic vision of the raw material,
> which can be fashioned by him relatively freely.[42]

---

[42] Quoted in Paul Arthur Schilpp and Maurice Friedman, eds., *The Philosophy of Martin Buber* (London: Open Court Publishing Company, 1967), p. 541.

The true educator must be able to select from the world whatever is necessary for this other person to achieve their fullness of being.[43] Our presence to our pupils then becomes a natural and spontaneous selection of the precise means necessary to cultivate the specific area of being for which we are responsible. This is where Buber differs from the perpetrators of 'progressive' education in the way these have been described by their enemies. The art of the teacher is selecting that portion of the world which will release the person of the child:

> Education, to Buber, means a conscious and willed 'selection of the effective world'. The teacher makes himself the living selection of the world, which comes in his person to meet, draw out, and form the pupil. In this meeting the teacher puts aside the will to dominate and enjoy the pupil, for this will more than anything else threatens to stifle the growth of his blessings. 'It must be one or the other,' writes Buber: 'Either he takes on himself the tragedy of the other person, and offers an unblemished daily sacrifice, or the fire enters his work and consumes it.'[44]

Response to a given situation with the whole of our life and being is what makes us educators. The response must be harmonised to the demands of the specific call. This implies knowledge of the situation, the pupils and the reality of education. It also forbids the selection of one's pupils:

> Eros is choice, choice made from inclination. This is precisely what education is not. The man who is loving in Eros chooses the beloved, the modern educator finds his pupil there before him. From this

---

[43] Friedman, *Martin Buber: The Life of Dialogue*, p. 181.
[44] Buber, *Israel and the World: Essays in a Time of Crisis*, quoted in Maurice Friedman, *Martin Buber: The Life of Dialogue*, p. 94.

unerotic situation the greatness of the modern
educator is to be seen – and most clearly when he is a
teacher. He enters the schoolroom for the first time,
he sees them crouching at the desks, indiscriminately
flung together, the misshapen and the well-
proportioned, animal faces, empty faces, and noble
faces in indiscriminate confusion, like the presence of
the created universe; the glance of the educator
accepts and receives them all.[45]

This glance of the educator is what the teacher must learn.
They must learn it so much by heart that it becomes natural
to them. This has been described in another context by
Antoine de Saint-Exupery:

Their fate causes these people no suffering. It is not
an impulse to charity that has upset me like this. I am
not weeping over an eternally open wound. Those
who carry the wound do not feel it. It is the human
race and not the individual that is wounded here, is
outraged here. I do not believe in pity. What torments
me is the gardener's point of view. What torments me
is not the poverty to which after all a man can
accustom himself as easily as to sloth. Generations of
Orientals live in filth and love it. What torments me
is not the humps nor the hollows nor the ugliness. It
is the sight, a little bit in all these men, of Mozart
murdered. Only the Spirit, if it breathe upon the clay,
can create Man.[46]

In Buber's view the spirit that must breathe upon the clay is
the unity of being of those teachers who are conscious of
their educational task. This consciousness requires that we

---

[45] Buber, *Between Man and Man*, p. 122.
[46] Antoine de Saint-Exupery, *Wind, Sand and Stars*, English translation
of *Terre des Hommes* (London: Penguin, 1966), pp. 183–4.

know ourselves and that we understand the particular being in front of us. The interest we take in this particular person must be the gardener's interest, which alone should inspire us. We cannot desire to impose on the other our own struggle for actualisation. We have to have achieved that unity of being before we begin to educate.

CHAPTER FIVE

Pat Clarke and Paulo Freire

Anyway, I keep picturing all these little kids playing some game in this big field of rye and all. Thousands of little kids, and nobody's around – nobody big, I mean – except me. And I'm standing on the edge of some crazy cliff. What I have to do, I have to catch everybody if they start to go over the cliff – I mean if they're running and they don't look where they're going I have to come out from somewhere and *catch* them. That's all I do all day. I'd just be the catcher in the rye and all. I know it's crazy, but that's the only thing I'd really like to be.[47]

Father Pat Clarke, an Irish Holy Ghost missionary, born in the Liberties in Dublin, has spent most of his life as a priest in South America. He lives in São Paulo, Brazil, one of the largest cities in the world, which has an estimated population of 20 million. A city that never sleeps and where skyscrapers, visible from every conceivable viewpoint, climb heavenwards not so much in prayer or praise for what is above as in disdain for what is below. For in and around, and often hidden from view, despite Brazil's international reputation as an emerging economic giant, the city is host to more than two thousand favelas with a combined population of over one million people, as well as other large slum conglomerations called *corticos*, which are large houses with twenty or thirty rooms, each of which houses one family.

Favela is a Portuguese word for the wood from which the shacks are made. These makeshift dwellings are of course

---

[47] J. D. Salinger, *The Catcher in the Rye* (1951; London: Penguin, 1967), pp. 179–80.

made from many other materials, usually what people can find discarded on dumps or in scrapyards. In recent years, with the increase in personal and collective awareness (what Paulo Freire calls 'conscientisation'), due to the work of basic Christian communities and grassroots organisations, people's self-esteem and confidence has grown. Consequently, they are now able to engage in the struggle for a home worthy of the name, and a society in which they are no longer regarded as outcasts. But there is a long, hard road ahead to such a utopia, even in a country with such natural, mineral and human resources.

The economic model of development, in vogue since the industrial revolution in Europe and now exported to the rest of the world, generates progress and well-being at one level, but as much misery and exclusion at another. It is not a model of inclusion. So many of the assets and resources of the planet – such as air, water, forestry, biodiversity, mineral resources, culture and the wealth of basic human institutions – are regarded not only as infinite in quantity but as fodder to be plundered for dubious progress and an unparalleled obsession with money and profit at any cost.

There are therefore serious critical reasons to carefully examine what is called progress in Brazil or in any of the so-called emerging countries like China, India, South Africa, Mozambique, Angola, where huge sections of the populations are not only outside the 'wonder' of all this newfound wealth, but destined never to be part of it. And in a place like Brazil, it explains why the structural reality of the country, despite the desire of its current president to abolish poverty once and for all, is a gaping wound on the side of 'progress'.

In Sao Paulo, Fr Pat Clarke began his work in 1977 in the favela of Vila Prudente, one of the largest and oldest in the city. Then it was a sprawling network of alleyways, nearly all of them open-air, rat-infested sewers, straddled by railway sleepers that served as mini-bridges, along the edges of which children played all day. In the wooden shacks that stood along the edges of the sewers, families of five, eight, sometimes twelve people lived in one or two rooms, separated from neighbours by paper-thin walls. Gun-carrying gangs patrolled the place and deaths by shooting were common. On one occasion Fr Pat Clarke was himself held up in his car at gunpoint by a ten-year-old child who told him to hand over his money or have his brains blown out. This became a turning point in his apostolate. He had to do something to save the children. How do children in this situation get the opportunity to express themselves? The answer is simple: give them the means to do so. The big question for someone like Pat Clarke was, where do I possibly begin in a place like this? Two things came to the rescue: the Legion of Mary and the famous Brazilian philosopher of education, Paulo Freire.

The Legion of Mary had been in Vila Prudente long before Pat Clarke arrived. How and when it arrived is not recorded. But what it did was serve as a conduit for people to come together in their shacks, primarily as a faith community, and in time as a people with many other concerns that were articulated only slowly and usually with great diffidence. Pat Clarke's challenge was to try to encourage the articulation of these concerns as part of the people's understanding of their faith. Faith in a god who had given them the power to change situations that seemed at the time to be beyond both their understanding and their capacity to intervene. It was out of this 'faith–life' synthesis that the first major breakthrough came: the implantation of a sewage system that would eliminate the rivers of disease and hopelessness that surrounded the life of this community. It was at this point that Paulo Freire's philosophy came into play.

Pat Clarke had met Paulo Freire at an international seminar in Paris in 1974, when he was in exile and working at the World Council of Churches in Geneva. Five years later, he returned to Brazil with other exiles who had been granted an amnesty by the military government of the time. It was then that the two met up again, a meeting that was to be decisive for the ensuing work in Sao Paulo's favelas and in particular, Favela Vila Prudente. Paulo's methodology, though complex and elaborate, could be summed up by a few basic concepts. His advice to anyone going into areas of poverty and abandonment was simple: don't go with a ready-made project under your arm. Listen to the people, listen as if you respected them, listen to their vocabulary and note the dominant words they use. Out of that, you can construct a synthesis of their world – their concerns, their dreams, their culture, their values, their fears. Walk with them, not in front or behind them, but with them. And remember that everyone who teaches is also a learner, and every learner is also a teacher.

This was the philosophy that joined forces with the 'faith' of the people and led to the elimination of the rat-infested sewers, the building of a community centre, the building of a crèche, the beginning of an experiment with the arts which led to the foundation of the Centre for Art and Culture, which has become a utopia of transformation, both personal and collective, for the eighty children enrolled there at any given time and for their parents and the wider community. Since then, a pastoral centre has been added, dedicated to the name of the murdered archbishop of San Salvador, Oscar Romero, who is a figure of inspiration and hope for many struggling communities throughout Latin America. And in the last two years there is a new chapel, decorated artistically by the children and stunning in its simplicity. Youth contributed to the design by creating tiles and artwork for the centre, increasing their sense of ownership over the space. Local teenagers combed the nearby rubbish tips for broken tiles and glass bottles. These have been used to create beautiful mosaics that make up the façade of the buildings. So popular have the bottle-dashed frontages become that others living in the area have commissioned the teenagers to decorate their houses similarly. It is becoming a business offshoot of the art centre. Art is the way towards self-expression for otherwise voiceless young Brazilians. Art should be for everyone but we have to build a bridge somewhere between the place where each person is and the sophisticated world of the art gallery. That bridge begins in personal experience and the most basic opportunity for self-expression though some form of art.

What Pat Clarke is doing is obviously only a drop in the ocean. His multifaceted art school touches only a small number of the millions of children, many of whom die before they are eighteen. 'The waste of life is shocking,' he agrees, 'but despair would be to look merely at the statistics. Hope is to look at the metaphor, to look at the mosaic of life. If I take this piece out of the mosaic and leave it on its own, nobody would know what it is, it is only when I put it back into the total picture that it becomes intelligible.' As a teacher-learner though, you have to be a fly on the wall, says Fr Clarke, quoting Paulo Freire. You have to be a listener. Only then can you discover how to bring great music and art, which is the inheritance of humanity, to where it has never been heard of and make it part of a repertoire that includes the first artistic intuitions and experiments of a local culture, without destroying or debasing it. Visiting artists have helped this process and several works of the centre have been displayed in chic restaurants and galleries. 'Creativity is a mystery,' Fr Clarke tells us, 'and it's there for the tapping. Who can become an artist? When do I become an artist? It is the creative mystery that is in everyone and it is basic to all that we do here. It is the dream of being able to stand up and say: I am.'[48]

Paulo Freire's *Pedagogy of the Oppressed* is a study of education in the third world. Its findings, however, can be of vital interest to any educational situation:

There is no such thing as a *neutral* educational process. Education either functions as an instrument

---

[48] Fr Pat Clarke, *Where 2+2=5* (DVD), Esperanza Productions, 2007.

which is used to facilitate the integration of the younger generation into the logic of the present system and being about conformity to it, *or* it becomes 'the practice of freedom', the means by which men and women deal critically and creatively with reality and discover how to participate in the transformation of their world. The development of an education methodology that facilitates this process will inevitably lead to tension and conflict within our society. But it could also contribute to the formation of a new man and mark the beginning of a new era in Western history. For those who are committed to that task and are searching for concepts and tools for experimentation, Paulo Freire's thought may make a significant contribution in the years ahead.[49]

Freire's work is not the result of thought and study alone; it is rooted in concrete situations. His experience of teaching illiterate and oppressed people in Latin America has made him particularly sensitive to the specific psychology of the oppressed, the multiform forces of oppression, and the methods necessary to release the one from the other. 'The central problem is this,' he says, 'how can the oppressed, as divided, unauthentic beings, participate in developing the pedagogy of their liberation?' And he answers: 'Only as they discover themselves to be "the hosts" of the oppressor can they contribute to the midwifery of their liberating pedagogy.'

He analyses the socio-political and economic forces which have constituted the psychology of the oppressed and shows that these forces of oppression have become a whole culture in the third world. This culture prevents these people from ever releasing themselves from oppression: in their psychology these forces have been interiorised, they are part

---

[49] Richard Shaull, Foreword, Paulo Freire's *Pedagogy of the Oppressed* (London: Penguin, 1972), p. 14.

of the atmosphere in which they live. To release the oppressed from their way of being is not as easy as removing the forces of oppression. The socio-political situation in the third world has created a psychology and an atmosphere which combine to form the culture of the oppressed. The oppressed are a kind of people. Using the famous tyrant–slave analogy, Freire adds his own perceptive observations and concludes that there is a mentality of oppressed peoples, one that can be studied and must be studied if any 'pedagogy' is to be successful.

Freire spells out the alphabet of this mentality in ways that can help us understand our own educational problems as well. The whole structure of Western civilisation is one of domination and this means that any educational theory issuing from it is one that seeks to integrate the younger generation into the logic of its system, which means in turn that the pattern of all our pedagogy is propaganda. In the twenty-first century, instead of using education to harness our children to the status quo, we should be trying to develop an educational methodology which will free each person of the younger generation so that each one can deal critically and creatively with the unforeseeable reality ahead.

Paulo Freire's study of the fringe situation in the most oppressed regions of our cultural world provides us with an enlarged version of the concrete situation of every member of the younger generation. Father Pat Clarke's Centro Cultural Vila Prudente in Sao Paulo gives us an object lesson in how to initiate the process. Given the physical and psychological dependence of children and the cultural prejudices of the adult world, it follows that what Freire describes at a socio-political level in the underdeveloped countries can be used analogously to describe the situation of every pupil in the educational relationship. Richard Shaull suggests the same idea in the foreword to the 1972 edition of Freire's book:

In the United States, we are gradually becoming aware of the work of Paulo Freire, but thus far we have thought of it primarily in terms of its contribution to the education of illiterate adults in the third world. If, however, we take a closer look, we may discover that his methodology as well as his educational philosophy are as important for us as for the dispossessed in Latin America ... The sharpness and intensity of that struggle in the developing world may well provide us with new insight, new models, and a new hope as we face our own situation ... Paulo Freire's thought represents the response of a creative mind and sensitive conscience to the extraordinary misery and suffering of the oppressed around him ... There are certain parallels in the two situations which should not be overlooked. Our advanced technological society is rapidly making objects of most of us and subtly programming us into conformity to the logic of its system. To the degree that this happens we are also becoming submerged in a new 'culture of silence' ... The educational system is one of the major instruments for the maintenance of this culture of silence ... The young perceive that their right to say their own words has been stolen from them, and that few things are more important than the struggle to win it back. And they also realise that the educational system today – from kindergarten to university – is their enemy.[50]

Apart from one specific reference to Martin Buber in his text, and the inclusion of *I and Thou* in the bibliography, there are at least two chapters devoted to 'dialogue' and 'anti-dialogue' in education. Here the dialogical theories of both thinkers are remarkably similar. Such headings as 'the "banking" concept of education as an instrument of

---

[50] Ibid., pp. 11–14.

oppression'; 'the problem-posing concept of education as an instrument for liberation'; 'education as a world-mediated mutual process'; 'man as a consciously incomplete being, and his attempt to be more fully human'; and 'dialogics: the essence of education as the practice of freedom' reveal a striking parallel between the thought and aims of both Freire and Buber. The passages I shall quote from one author to support each point could, in every case, pass off as a quotation from the other. The first point of agreement is the unqualified condemnation of all forms of oppression in education:

'The real struggle', Buber said one day, 'is not between East and West, or capitalism and communism, but between education and propaganda. Education means teaching people to see the reality around them, to understand it for themselves, propaganda is exactly the opposite. It tells the people, "you will think like this, as we want you to think!"

'Education lifts the people up. It opens their hearts and develops their minds, so that they can discover the truth and make it their own. Propaganda, on the other hand, closes their hearts and stunts their minds. It compels them to accept dogmas without asking themselves, "Is this true or not?"

'The trouble is that this is not only a conflict of ideology. It is a conflict of tempo. The tempo of propaganda is feverish, nervous ... whereas education goes at a slow pace. It is the pace of teacher talking with their pupils. It is the pace of a man reading by himself in a room. It cannot be hurried and speeded up and remain education.'[51]

---

[51] Buber, quoted in Aubrey Hodes, *Encounter with Martin Buber* (London: Penguin, 1975), p. 135.

This harmful concept of education is widespread and is present, sometimes unobtrusively, in all educational contact in our Western civilisation. It is the political attitude of domination, the colonial mentality of the 'civilising' conqueror of the world:

> The desire for conquest (or rather the necessity of conquest) is at all times present in anti-dialogical action. To this end the oppressors attempt to destroy in men their quality as 'considerers' of the world. Since the oppressors cannot totally achieve this destruction, they must *mythicize* the world. In order to present for the consideration of the oppressed and subjugated a world of deceit designed to increase their alienation and passivity, the oppressors develop a series of methods precluding any presentation of the world as a problem and showing it as a fixed entity, as something given – something to which men, as spectators, must adapt ... The internalisation of these myths is essential to the subjugation of the oppressed ... All domination involves invasion – at times physical and overt, at times camouflaged, with the invader assuming the role of helping friend ... For cultural conquest to succeed, it is essential that those invaded become convinced of their intrinsic inferiority.[52]

Both authors would agree about the nature and the extent of anti-dialogical education. They would also agree about the first step to be taken in the other direction:

> In its first stage the pedagogy must deal with the problem of the consciousness of the oppressed and the oppressor ... It must take into account their behaviour, their view of the world, and their ethics ... Any situation in which A objectively exploits B or

---

[52] Freire, *Pedagogy of the Oppressed*, pp. 109–10, 121–2.

hinders his pursuit of self-affirmation as a responsible person is one of oppression. Such a situation in itself constitutes violence ... because it interferes with man's ontological and historical vocation to be more fully human.[53]

The third point upon which both would agree is that the opposite of oppression is not freedom. It is communion. This is what must be achieved in the education which is *to* freedom, but not *through* freedom. The fact is that the oppressed are incapable of freedom. They fear it and are unable to reach it unless the necessary therapeutic arrangements are made by the educator. They cannot reach it on their own. Nor can it be imposed on them. Only 'those in communion liberate one another'.[54] This quotation from Freire could so easily be from Martin Buber.

The fourth point on which they agree is that the pupil must, at all times, be a conscious participator in his or her own education. The first step must come from them. No one can be educated in spite of themselves:

Critical and liberating dialogue ... must be carried on with the oppressed at whatever stage their struggle for liberation has reached. The content of that dialogue can and should vary in accordance with historical conditions and the level at which the oppressed perceive reality. But to substitute monologue ... for dialogue is to try to liberate the oppressed with the instruments of domestication ... It is necessary to trust in the oppressed and their ability to reason. Whoever lacks this trust will fail to bring about (or abandon) dialogue, reflection and communication.[55]

---

[53] Ibid., p. 31.
[54] Ibid., p. 103.
[55] Ibid., p. 41.

Freire and Buber agree that the first step must be the pupil's. The work of the educator is to make it possible. We must understand the being of the pupil so well that we forestall their 'resistance against being educated'. We must provide the kind of direct contact with the pupil that will reach them effectively. We will have to understand all that lies between us and the pupil, and have the 'imagination' to aim this relation in whatever way is likely to circumvent all these obstacles.

Traditional education is an instrument that integrates the younger generation into the logic of the prevailing system. A cultural and psychological atmosphere is generated which produces in the young person the mentality common to all those who are in a situation of dependence upon a more powerful and dominating race. To achieve the fundamental aim of fitting our youth into the system we have perfected over the years, it is essential that such a mentality should be encouraged in them:

> The conqueror imposes his objectives on the vanquished, and makes them his possession. He imposes his own contours on the vanquished, who internalise this shape and become ambiguous beings 'housing' another.[56]

This ambiguity is the first factor essential to an understanding of the mentality of the student. It is the keystone to the success of traditional education, which is structured around the fearful obedience of the pupil to the many precepts of the master. It matters little whether this obedience is cultivated by a reign of terror or a more subtle campaign of secret influence; the task is the same and the mentality upon which it grafts itself is also similar:

---

[56] Ibid., p. 108.

The oppressed suffer from the duality which has established itself in their innermost being. They discover that without freedom they cannot exist authentically. Yet, although they desire authentic existence, they fear it. They are at one and the same time themselves and the oppressor whose consciousness they have internalised. The conflict lies in the choice between being wholly themselves or being divided; between ejecting the oppressor within or not ejecting him; between human solidarity or alienation; between following prescriptions or having choices; between being spectators or actors; between acting or having illusion of acting through the action of the oppressors; between speaking out or being silent, castrated in their power to transform the world.[57]

This is the situation of the Gradgrind children in Dickens' novel *Hard Times*. The only worldview they know is the one prescribed for them by their father. Apart from this 'world', there is nothing. And they are tired of this world. It may be the only 'logical' one, the only one offering the security of a coherent structure, but it does not answer to the deep yearnings that stir in their souls. Obviously, they are ashamed of these foreign impulses which they cannot deny but which they are forced to condemn because no credence is given to them in the worldview of the oppressor. The children are helpless. They have neither the strength, the courage, nor the competence to articulate these hidden factors into a coherent statement of fact requiring confrontation. There are two possibilities: they either quench this hidden side of themselves and adopt the worldview of the oppressor, or they take the fearful step towards freedom and condemn themselves to isolated insecurity. Instead of helping the child to overcome the

---

[57] Ibid., pp. 24–5.

innate fear of freedom which invades the psychology of every young person, traditional education capitalises on this fear. Feeding this fear and insecurity with every means at their disposal, the traditional educator saw it as their role, in the preservation and maintenance of civilised society, to turn the child's natural fear into an internalised guardian of the peace. Only when the exterior forces of oppression have been replaced by an equally competent internalised version of themselves, can we be sure that the ordered system of society will be perpetuated. To prevent the destructive originality of every person born into the world from corroding the fabric of 'civilised community living', it is essential to castrate this originality by so augmenting the natural fear of it in the child that they crush it out altogether. This is easily done if the children are taken at an early age and encouraged to reject their own incoherent impulses in favour of the worldview of their 'elders and betters'.

The success and the permanence of 'traditional' society depended upon a conspiracy to promote this castration process. Parents, teachers, society itself, were both the victims and the perpetrators of this logical system:

> As authoritarian relations between parents and children intensify, children in their infancy increasingly internalise parental authority ... Internalising parental authority through the rigid relationship structure emphasised by the school, these young people tend when they become professionals (because of the very fear of freedom instilled by these relationships) to repeat the rigid pattern in which they were miseducated.[58]

There is no doubt that this system makes for efficient and organised civilisation. It produces a society which can perpetuate itself consistently and achieve a very high standard

---

[58] Ibid., pp. 123–4.

of living. A collectivity of individuals is certainly an improvement on anarchy and chaos. The promoters of 'progressive' education, based exclusively upon the development of the originator instinct in children, are trying to fight for the cause of freedom by simply removing the external forces of oppression. The weakness of this movement is its failure to analyse sufficiently the causes of oppression. It fails to see that a new situation would have to be established within which the vocation to freedom could be achieved. Without positive and creative forces working towards this end, the most important of which is the person of the teacher, freedom can never emerge. And anarchy and chaos are even less desirable than domination and imposed order.

But the question is this: does this imposed order provide the framework adequate to fulfilment as a unique and complete being? And the answer is that this kind of life is bought at too high a price. It demands the sacrifice of genuine personhood and stands between us and our self-realisation as beings. The education which could act as substitute for the 'traditional' system is one which would hope to salvage as many of the advantages of the older kind as are consonant with its primary aim, but it declares that sacrifice of personal being is too high a price to pay for any kind of life however comfortable or efficient. Each one of us is capable of a personal form of existence towards which every educational effort must strive. Unless we accede to this dimension, our education is a failure. We must abandon all education of domination and propaganda. If we agree that any education which is the imposition of an already existing pattern of life, from outside and from above, upon another person is a system of oppression, and if we agree that the early insertion of children into a system of education which moulds them into a predetermined pattern of life, however laudable or beautiful, is a system of oppression, then we must turn away from this to whatever possibilities can open up the pastures of our personal freedom.

The basic premise of this education to freedom is that it must begin with the child. It is a growth that is nurtured and directed by the educator, but which must find its roots in the person being educated. This implies that it cannot be 'hurried or speeded up and remain education'. Both its being and its time must come from the student.

> As historical, autobiographical, 'beings for themselves', their transformation [development] occurs in their own existential time, never outside it.[59]

This is what Buber calls 'the truth of the slower tempo'. Progress in education can only be measured in terms of the real growth of the person in question. The possibility of such growth is facilitated by genuine educational contact with the person of the teacher. This contact is what gives the child confidence in themselves and trust in the meaning of the world. Once this confidence has been established the child is ready to ask. In asking they are trying out the ground under their feet. Once the trust has been established, the teacher can promote and direct the growth of the child, whether that growth be intellectual, psychological, emotional or spiritual, by simply being present and allowing the children to pit their strength, their curiosity, their fear and their desire against the more resilient mettle of the teacher's already fashioned character. The educational encounter is not one that dominates or absorbs. It is the meeting between character and character. The unity of being which gives the teacher real presence and makes of them 'the Great Character', or whatever approximation of this they may have achieved, is the magnet and the sounding board that draws out the child and fashions their own character. There may be conflict or confirmation between them, but, in this educational arena, it is not the content of the meeting but rather the meeting itself which truly educates.

---

[59] Ibid., p. 129.

To make the educational contact truly liberating it must move through at least three decisive stages. The first is a readiness on the part of the teacher to allow him or her self to be a leaning-post in the initial steps towards autonomy. The pupil is attracted towards the teacher in the way that every oppressed person is inevitably drawn towards the oppressor. Without taking advantage of this natural attraction, the teacher must use it to promote the growth of his charge. This is done by responding in a way that will allow the students to come out of their shell, but, at the same time, will allow them to be, later on, cured of this cure itself. Thus, the second step in the movement is to make the student aware of the mechanism of their own liberation process. The third step is the student's final recovery not just from the disease but also from the treatment. Only when the student has finally assumed the independent weight of their own person is the educational process complete.

In other words, the educational programme is neither the propaganda of the traditional system, nor is it the spurious freedom of anarchy. It is a liberating structure which preserves the integrity of its essential aim by inserting the person of the teacher as the keystone, thereby replacing the refractory kernel of a system with the mercurial element of a person. The role of the teacher is to maintain the paradox of a 'structure towards freedom'.

Although the situation demands that the teacher 'carry out the education of character indirectly', this does not allow him or her to act 'surreptitiously'. There can be no politics in education, even if it is successfully hidden. 'Even if the pupil does not detect it, it falsifies the teacher ... Only the totality of the teacher, with his whole involuntary existence, affects the totality of the pupil.' This process of education must become 'natural' to the teacher. Although they are required to examine their situation with care and precision, although they are called to practice 'a lofty asceticism', neither of these will have any effect unless both are assumed into a transformation of the total being of the teacher which makes of him or her a genuine educator. This ever-recurring paradox of the 'willing' yet 'involuntary' presence of the educator has been expressed enigmatically by Buber: 'It is that which we will when we, educating without wilfulness, will.'[60] Put less pithily, this suggests that when we as teachers feel ourselves sufficiently sure of our natural and spontaneous being, we are able to put this wholeness willingly and consciously into the educational process and our very assurance awakens the trust of the student and allows the genuine educational relationship to happen. To achieve this 'natural tact' of the educator it is important that we understand the comprehensive specificity of our unique situation and the precise realm of being for which we are responsible. This knowledge will allow us to form the habit that will make our presence to our pupils a spontaneous and essentially educational contact. This also demands that we be fully aware of the student's dependence upon us, and our role as 'hero' in the initial stages of the educational encounter.

> Teaching is an existential encounter that results in a radical change of character ... In this sense the teacher is a hero, albeit a hero in the common usage of the word. He is someone the student looks up to and admires, someone he emulates, someone he tries to follow. The student is enthralled by the teacher, he is spiritually captured by him. Where this is not the case, the so-called teacher holds no real authority; for to possess the authority implies the willingness of the student to give over a part of his freedom to the teacher.[61]

---

[60] Martin Buber, *Gleanings*, *The Philosophy of Martin Buber*, Paul Arthur Schillip and Maurice Friedman, eds. (London: Open Court, 1967), p. 101.
[61] Gary S. Belkin, 'The Teacher as Hero', *Educational Theory* 22 (Autumn 1972), p. 416.

The educational situation is one of thraldom. Without this power and this need it lacks the magnetism necessary to draw the child out. The peculiar 'thraldom' is the result of contact between the formed adult and the unformed child. It is a major force in education if it is understood and regulated by the teacher. It is the product of youthful psychology and the mentality of the oppressed:

At a certain point in their existential experience the oppressed feel an irresistible attraction towards the oppressor and his way of life. Sharing his way of life becomes an overpowering aspiration. In their alienation, the oppressed want at any cost to resemble the oppressor, to imitate him, to follow him.[62]

This dependence of the oppressed upon the oppressor can be applied to the situation of any young person in his relations with those of his teachers who have the power to influence. Without this power and authority, education lacks any cohesive growth-promoting structure. Freud, as early as 1914, explicitly stated that teachers' function, at a psychological level, was to act as substitute fathers and mothers, and that the attitudes of children towards them derive from attitudes towards their own parents, which have been developed in infancy and childhood.[63] Jung confirms this also in his essay on 'Child Development and Education':

In this battle for freedom the school plays a not unimportant part, as it is the first milieu the child finds outside his home. School comrades take the place of brothers and sisters; the teacher, if a man, acts as substitute for the father, and, if a woman, for the mother. It is important that the teacher should be

---

[62] Freire, *Pedagogy of the Oppressed*, p. 38.
[63] C. G. Jung, 'Some Reflections on Schoolboy Psychology', *Complete Works*, Vol. XIII (London: Hogarth Press, 1955).

conscious of the role he is playing. He must not be satisfied with merely pounding the curriculum into the child; he must also influence him through his personality. This latter function is at least as important as the actual teaching, if not more so in certain cases.[64]

If this situation of dependence is to be transformed into one of freedom and personal responsibility, it must be thoroughly understood by the teacher. What each teacher must realise is that their responsibility is to release the student and not to either exploit them or prolong their natural state of dependence. Education based on the will to power or Eros thrives upon the thraldom which the educational situation generates. The teacher either enjoys the power which he or she exercises or else they exploit it to mould the oppressed into an image of themselves. The work of genuine educational contact, on the other hand, is to use the natural dependence of the pupil in a way that will allow for full development of independent personality. This can be achieved by inaugurating a critical and liberating dialogue with the students which will reveal to them their own situation. It will be achieved more positively by the gradual interpolation of a liberating structure between the student and the teacher.

The initial dependence is good if it inspires in the student a trust of the teacher. It means that the student is ready to do what the teacher suggests. The genuine educator will see that this trust is honoured.

They will provide the student with the wherewithal to detach themselves from this dependence. They will organise it so that the students are led to encounter other things besides the teacher. They will use this power over the student to lead them to an appreciation of the world that

[64] C. G. Jung, 'The Development of Personality', *Collected Works*, Vol. 17, Bollingen Series XX, #55.

mediates between them. They will gradually replace their own pivotal place in the child's life by an ever-increasing deflection of the centre of gravity towards the child's own centre:

> Those who work for liberation must not take advantage of the emotional dependence of the oppressed ... Libertarian action must recognise this dependence as a weak point and must attempt through reflection and action to transform it into independence.[65]

There are two ways of taking advantage of this emotional dependence. The first is by enjoying it; the second is by employing it to further one's own ends. In the first case the teacher enjoys and revels in the emotional dependence of the child. There is something very attractive about being needed to the extent of becoming the source of an almost irresistible power in the life of any other being. The question is not whether the teacher feels this power and enjoys exercising it, but whether he or she uses it for the desire to enthral. Unless this power becomes legitimate educational influence it is just one more source of depersonalisation.

The fact that this situation can be abused must not blind us to its rich potentiality. If we as educators are capable of genuine educational contact then we can turn this power of thraldom into the most fruitful source of growth for our students. We do this by acting as midwife between their being as unformed individuals and the full realisation of their independent personhood. The three moments in such growth towards freedom are trust, confirmation and liberation.

The trust which makes up the basis of 'every true existential relationship between two persons' must not be

---

[65] Freire, *Pedagogy of the Oppressed*, p. 42.

naïve. It must take into account the mentality of the oppressed which sometimes betrays it. The betrayal is not malicious. It is simply the result of that insecurity and ambiguity which we have detected in the psychology of all dependent and oppressed peoples:

> This confidence should not be naïve. The leaders must believe in the potentialities of the people ... but they must always mistrust the *ambiguity* of oppressed men, mistrust the oppressor 'housed' in the latter.[66]

Trust is not enough. There must also be confirmation. This implies a struggle and the possibility of opposition. The teacher must sometimes defend the pupils against themselves. The teacher must at times be an enemy, placing him or herself between the forces of oppression and the student in order to fight against both. This is the case where the student is not aware either of the danger to his or her own liberty or of the evil of their attachment to the forces of oppression. As genuine educators we must devote the whole of our being to the particular sphere for which we are responsible: the liberation of fullness of being in others. To do this we must establish a trust between ourselves and our students. But this does not allow us to confirm in them anything less than the truth of their own existence. We must not impose a truth. We must confirm the truth that issues from them in a confused and faltering way. We must teach them clearly what they are telling us confusedly about themselves. The initiative must come from them. The direction and the confirmation come from us. The relation of genuine educational contact is one that is mutual. It can never be accomplished without the participation of the student. At the same time it is never fully mutual. It is monitored by the teacher who assumes responsibility for the total relation. Through the working of our realistic

---

[66] Ibid., p. 137.

imagination we as teachers live the relationship from both sides. We work towards the effective liberation of the pupil from all oppressive forces that stand between them and the full flowering of their personality. Education worthy of the name, says Buber, is education of character.

Character is what allows the illusive reality of personality to spread into every pore of the total being of the student. It is what makes him or her exist fully as they are, by the full appropriation of their ownmost and unique form. This form can be elicited only by direct contact with the total being of another person. This contact may take the form of conflict. But it is not the content that is the primary word of education but, rather, the contact itself. If we as teachers have to set ourselves up in opposition to our charges, if we have to stand between them and themselves, or their interior version of 'the oppressor', then we must not shirk this responsibility. We must, at all times, be aware of the power we exercise and see that it is used as legitimate influence rather than as arbitrary domination or wilful enjoyment. We must use the power of thraldom which provides us with our effective authority in the educational situation, to coax the student towards a higher level of being, towards the assumption of responsibility for their own life and personality. We do this, not by suppressing or neglecting or underestimating the magnetism which we exercise over the unformed being that stands before us, but by using this influence in a way which will elevate their need before satisfying it.

The primary word of education is contact, contact between teacher and student. This contact is generated by a need the underdeveloped being has to attach himself to, and be dependent upon, another mature being. Time and magnetism are given to the teacher to establish a trust, to bring out the child, to release the child from all forces of oppression, to allow him or her to live their own life by the appropriation of their ownmost form, and not to be 'lived by' some other force. During this time the teacher should be filtering through to the child those selected elements of the world which he or she sees as most suited to the awakening of the child and the implementation of this meeting with the universe. If we are really teachers we will make the last movement of our teaching programme into a release of the child from its dependence on us. This cure will be the natural outcome of growth and critical, liberating dialogue. We will be able to show the child that this situation of dependence is a fundamental weakness that must be overcome, even for the good of our relationship. And we should have, during our teaching relationship, supplied the child with the elements necessary to break with this fruitful dependence so they may live fully their own lives.

After being invited to represent Ireland at the XXIV Sao Paulo Bienal, Brian Maguire arranged to spend eight weeks working at the Centro Cultural Vila Prudente during February and March of 1998. Maguire based his exhibition on the work at the centre. When he first made his submission to the authorities at the Bienal he was told that he could not bring the favela to the exhibition, so he began to achieve this goal in a roundabout manner. He gave art classes to the children who were coming to the centre and also did charcoal portraits of some of them, which they then took and hung in their homes. He was invited by the families to visit and to see his portraits hanging in their homes. He took photographs of these in situ. He also did portraits of many prisoners based on newspaper photographs of the overcrowded jails of the city. 'He had spent twelve years teaching art to convicts in Irish prisons, where he built up many close friendships and was consistently impressed by the basic humanity of the men he dealt with and by the mysterious problem, that each of them had somehow gotten himself into a trap. The Brazilian prisoners whose pictures he saw in the papers were also in the trap, and the economically and culturally deprived children he worked with at the Centro Cultural might be described as on their way to the trap.'[67] His final exhibition showed the direct connection between the children and the prisoners, the inevitable transformation of the one into the other because of 'the oppressor' housed in both as the socio-economic circumstances which surround everybody in Brazil. Art becomes the only pedagogy of the oppressed in this arena and the work of Fr Pat Clarke and the Centro Cultural Vila Prudente the only Catcher in the Rye standing between the children and their prison sentence. (Incidentally, some of the children whom Brian painted, now young adults, have become artists themselves.)

---

[67] Thomas McEvilley, Brian Maguire at the XXIV São Paulo Bienal, 3 October–13 December, 1998.

CHAPTER SIX

Mythic Intelligence

Once the direction ... was still known about. But that was a long time ago. And now there is no way you could even start to discover it again through reasoning, because reasoning is precisely what covered it over in the first place; is what did everything possible to obliterate its traces. The only way to find it is through your neglected sense of smell ... [not] smell that used to tell where your territory begins and someone else's ends, but about something even more instinctive: the scent of recognition, of rediscovering ancient links and affinities long forgotten ... And with this recognition comes sweetness – along with the knowledge that things will be simpler now. The hardest part is already over. The greatest struggle is behind us, and what lies ahead is like the joy of opening your mouth to rain or of running effortlessly down a gentle grassy slope.[68]

Kathleen Raine, who was born in 1908 and who died at the age of ninety-five in 2003, summed up herself and the century through which she had lived as follows:

A child of my time, who at Cambridge read Natural Sciences, and rejected my Christian heritage in order to adopt with uncritical zeal the current scientific orthodoxy of that university, I have lived long enough to come full circle. It is all that I learned in my Cambridge days that I have little by little come to reject, by a reversal of premises which has brought me to my own Orient. A slow learner, I have been blessed

---

[68] Peter Kingsley, *Reality* (Inverness, CA: The Golden Sufi Center, 2003), p. 317.

with a long life which has brought me to a knowledge
not taught in our schools.[69]

William Butler Yeats certainly believed in a knowledge of
another kind. He wrote in his preface to Lady Gregory's
Gods and Fighting Men (1904), 'Children at play, at being
great and wonderful people' are the true reality of what we
are and what we should become. 'Mankind as a whole had
a like dream once; everybody and nobody built up the
dream bit by bit and the storytellers are there to make us
remember.'[70] But the children of the twentieth century had
put away these ambitions for one reason or another; we
simply grew into ordinary men and women. How did this
happen? In 1926 Yeats wrote to Sturge Moore: 'As A. N.
Whitehead puts it: "The seventeenth century produced a
scheme of scientific thought framed by mathematicians for
the use of mathematicians."'[71]

We are symbolic animals. Whatever enters our head from
the outside world has to be translated into something else
that represents it inside. So, each object we envisage is
stripped of its material weight and size and texture and is
flashed on a screen inside our minds in a completely
dematerialised facsimile of itself. Everything we understand
or comprehend is received by us symbolically. Otherwise
our heads would be too heavy to sit on our shoulders. If I
ask you to think of a tree and you close your eyes and
imagine one, your tree and mine could be completely
different in shape and size: yours could look like a massive
oak with spreading leaves, mine could be a tall fir with
thickset greenery. How can both these images represent the

---

[69] Kathleen Raine, *W. B. Yeats and the Learning of the Imagination*
(Ipswich: Golgonooza Press, 1999), pp. 5–6.
[70] W. B. Yeats, Preface, Lady Augusta Gregory, *Gods and Fighting Men:
The Story of the Tuatha De Danaan and of the Fianna of Ireland* (London:
J. Murray, 1904).
[71] 27 May 1926, *W. B Yeats and T. Sturge Moore: Their Correspondence
1901–1937*. Ursula Bridge, ed. (London: Routledge and Paul, 1953).

same thing? And yet we understand both to be trees. I use a triangular form, you use a circular one to describe the reality which both of us recognise as trees in the world around us. Yet neither of our representations look anything like any trees we have ever seen in our lives. They don't look like each other, and they don't look like what they are meant to represent, yet they are symbols which we can both recognise. And that is the way our heads work. We cannot receive or transmit images in any other way. We receive the world and transmit it to one another in abstract symbols inside our minds.

When we imagine a tree in our minds we have both taken the geometrical outline of whatever tree springs to mind; as we say, we remove its material trappings, its branches, its leaves, its sap, its trunk, and we have reduced it to an abstract sketch of itself, an outline of its bulk. This is the kind of geometrical gymnastics which automatically goes on in our heads every minute of our daily lives. Geometry is, in this way, the most natural and fluent symbolism of the mind. We reduce most things to lines, angles, circles, cones, and then they can fit easily inside the confines of our brains. However, there are other kinds of symbolism and other ways for reality to gain access to our organisms. But these other ways of receiving reality are sometimes scorned by those who value the so-called 'scientific' way and who even sometimes refuse to accept that there are ways other than scientific for viewing the universe.

Consider what John Carey, Merton Professor at Oxford University and chair of the Man Booker judges for 2004, has to say about W. B. Yeats in a review of the first two volumes of Roy Foster's biography of the author. 'Was he, you find yourself blasphemously wondering, really that intelligent?' He goes on to list the usual proofs of intellectual backwardness:

He was substandard at school ... He never learnt to spell: even as a grown man, simple monosyllables

foxed him ... His gullibility was fathomless. Mysticism
and magic, to which he was introduced by the half-
batty George Russell, occupied much of his waking
and sleeping life. He believed he conversed with old
Celtic gods and a copious ragbag of other
supernaturals.[72]

It may be that only those, like W. B. Yeats, who have escaped
the trap of formal education are able to retain their
imaginative faculties by default. Each of us has been gifted
with a 'mythic' imagination, which we used extravagantly in
our childhood; but as we grew up we were taught to
abandon this way of entertaining the universe and forced to
channel everything through the narrow confines of logical
thinking.

Yeats's intelligence was essentially mythic. Such
intelligence weaves its way through symbols and has a very
different perspective on the universe to that of the scientist.
Richard Dawkins carries the following quote from John
Carey on his website and introduces it as follows:

Could science just be too difficult for some people,
and therefore seem threatening? Oddly enough, I
wouldn't dare to make such a suggestion, but I am
happy to quote a distinguished literary scholar, John
Carey, the present Merton Professor of English at
Oxford: 'The annual hordes competing for places on
arts courses in British universities, and the trickle of
science applicants, testify to the abandonment of
science among the young. Though most academics
are wary of saying it straight out, the general
consensus seems to be that arts courses are popular

---

[72] John Carey, 'Poetic License', review of R. F. Foster, *W. B. Yeats: A Life*,
Vol. I, 'The Apprentice Mage 1865–1914' (Oxford: Oxford University
Press, 1997); II, 'The Arch-Poet', 2003, *Sunday Times*, 9 March 1997, sec.
8, p. 1.

because they are easier, and that most arts students would simply not be up to the intellectual demands of a science course.'[73]

Here science and the scientific way of thinking are regarded as the norm and other ways of thinking are measured against these and found wanting. However, this is to overlook the possibility that there are other ways of knowing which are quite different from those emphasised and promoted to the exclusion of all others by our recent culture. To understand this reductionist vision of the brain we have to make a slight detour.

The human brain is the product of at least 500 million years of evolution in vertebrate animals. All vertebrates have a central nervous system – a spinal cord and a brain – in which sensations come together and responses originate. The first structures and functions of the brain to develop have not changed very much. But as the brain evolved, new structures and functions were added to the basic elements. As we walk around the world today, there are three parts to our brain, or, if we want to maintain the overall unity of our minds, we could say that our brains are tripartite. The older part continues to function today in much the same way it did for our ancestors millions of years ago. Since then we have developed two more storeys on top of this basic original structure. Although the primitive part remains active and true to itself, our total being is transformed by the two other layers which have been placed over this. It is important to stress that all three parts of the brain remain interconnected, even though our contemporary world acts as if we had nothing but the topmost layer, where abstract thinking presides.

The hindbrain is the oldest and the one we share with reptiles. It is a bulbous elaboration of the spinal cord, almost a carbuncle on the *medulla oblongata*. This is the serpentine

---

[73] www.edge.org/3rd_culture/dawkins/lecture_p6.html.

brain which reacts without second thought to uncomfortable situations the moment they occur. It takes care of our primal instincts and our most basic functions, our breathing and our heartbeat, for instance. Instincts for survival, dominance and mating are from this area of the brain. Steeped in the physiology of survival, the reptilian brain is the one still functioning once we are pronounced 'brain dead.' If the reptilian brain dies, the rest of the body will follow; the other two brains are less essential to the neurology of sustaining life. As you can imagine, this antediluvian brain has motivations more suited to asocial carnivores than to etiquette in polite society. And sometimes we allow it to manifest itself in the most inappropriate ways and places.

One of the more recent manifestations of it has been recognised as 'road rage', which only became known in the United States in the 1980s, and from as early as 1997 therapists have been working to have it certified as a medical condition, so that we can continue to make threats, insult or verbally abuse one another on the motorway when overcome by an explosive disorder. Classifying such outbursts as a 'medical condition' would let us off the hook for behaviour which we should be able to control and for which we should be held accountable. In other words, so-called 'road rage' becomes a symbol and a symptom of our failure to acknowledge, encounter and educate the snake inside ourselves. Our educational system has to provide the means by which we can come to terms with our ever-present serpentine brain.

The second part of the brain spread itself over the first. We sometimes call it the 'limbic system,' the 'emotional' or 'old mammalian' brain. As the name implies, it is the layer that evolved when we left our lives among the reptiles and developed into mammals. It evolved in our more primitive mammalian ancestors about 150 million years ago. It is where our emotions reside, and where memory begins. The two of these combine to produce in us positive or negative feelings.

Snakes apparently don't have either memory or emotion. They neither like nor remember you. The great divide between the serpents and the mammals has to do with the way they produce their offspring. The reptile lays eggs and slithers away indifferently. The mammal produces its young inside itself and develops a relationship with it. Mammals nourish and safeguard their young from the hostile world outside.[74] As we split off from the reptilian line, 'a fresh neural structure blossomed within our skulls'. This brand-new brain transformed not just the mechanics of reproduction but also the way we related to our offspring. We got all emotional and began to fuss about our young. The limbic system (or paleomammalian brain) is a set of brain structures which has also been called 'the visceral brain'. Though inarticulate and unreasoning, it can be expressive and intuitive. It is in this part of the brain that we sense the world mythically and where poetry is the *lingua franca*, because here we are living the world symbolically. Obviously the tripartite brain has to function harmoniously to produce articulate results from each of its layers, but the visceral brain is the mover and the shaker when it comes to poetry and mythic endeavour, while the rest of the brain acts simply as a fountainhead for this cornucopia.

Moving towards the later brain, the third storey, which is where we can express ourselves in clear-cut abstract fashion, the newest part of the brain (*neocortex* – Greek for 'new' and Latin for 'rind' or 'bark') is the last, and, in humans, the largest of the three brains. Dogs and cats, for instance, have more of this cortex than other mammals, and monkeys even more still. But in us human beings, the neocortex has ballooned to massive proportions. Because of this expansiveness, the brain needs such head room that we now have to wait until we are outside the womb to allow its extensive accommodation to develop fully. For this to

74 Thomas Lewis, M.D., Fari Amini, M.D., Richard Lannon, M.D., *A General Theory of Love* (New York: Vintage Books, 2000), p. 25.

happen we have to be born before our time. We have to emerge from the womb before our heads have developed to full capacity. Otherwise our big heads would prevent us from exiting through the given escape route. As Dr Stuart Shanker further explains: 'Babies are born with a brain that is one quarter of the size of their adult brain; in a sense, compared to other species human babies are born prematurely in that they have a very long period of complete reliance on their primary caregiver (usually the mother) for their survival.'[75] Human beings have the largest neocortex-to-brain ratio of any creature, an inequitable proportion that confers upon us our capacity to reason. The jurisdiction of will is also limited to this latest brain and to those functions within its purview. So you can see how easy it was for the neocortex to assume that it was in charge and that it could control all the other monsters lurking in the deep.

The problem is that we came so enamoured and intoxicated by our most recent development scheme that we neglected and forgot the other two basic elements of our cranial make-up. We moved everything into the top storey and began living there as if this penthouse were the whole enchilada.

Evolution is 'a kaleidoscope, not a pyramid'.[76] Scientists warn us against buying into a simplistic version of a most mysterious and complex system. 'Many people conceive of evolution as an upward staircase, an unfolding sequence that produces ever more advanced organisms.'[77] Such warnings should prevent us from either overemphasising

---

[75] Dr Shanker is a distinguished Research Professor of Philosophy and Psychology at York University and currently serving as director of the Milton and Ethel Harris Research Initiative, whose goal is to build on new knowledge of the brain's development, and help set children (including those with developmental disorders) on the path towards emotional and intellectual health.

[76] Lewis, Amini and Lannon, *A General Theory of Love*, p. 30.

[77] Ibid.

the importance of the latest version, or dismissing or undervaluing the ever-present reptilian component of the brain. 'The neocortical brain is not the most advanced of the three, but simply the most recent.'[78]

We have practically dismissed the two first parts of the brain in our educational system and concentrated our attention on the last, the neocortex. There should be a sympathetic and complementary relationship between all three parts of the brain but, unfortunately, the neocortex finds the other two far too slow-moving and dim-witted to be taken seriously and so this third and last part of the brain is inclined to ignore the signals coming from the other two and to carry on with the exciting work of explaining the universe on its own terms.

The neocortex should spend at least some of its time and all of its attention during that time to listening to the prompts coming from the other two parts of the brain. Often, admittedly, the transition from impulse to idea is a difficult and frustrating passage, as we must strain to force a strong feeling into the straitjacket of verbal expression. We have to squeeze our feelings and emotions through the tiny hubcap at the top of our head. The result of such a combination is often called 'poetry,' a bridge between the neocortical and limbic brains, which begins, according to Robert Frost, 'as a lump in the throat, a sense of wrong, a homesickness, a love sickness. It is never a thought to begin with.'[79]

We need all three components of our brain, and our maturity involves the correct balance afforded to each one of the three. Because, essentially, the three are designed to interrelate. 'Each brain has evolved to interdigitate with its cranial cohabitants.'[80] However, this is not what has

---

[78] Ibid., pp. 30–1.
[79] Louis Untermeyer, ed., *The Letters of Robert Frost to Louis Untermeyer* (New York: Holt, Rinehart & Winston, 1963), p. 22.
[80] Lewis, Amini and Lannon, *A General Theory of Love*, p. 31.

happened. We live in a world which has completely discarded the first two parts of the brain and which overemphasises the third. Why not? It gives us our capacity to reason and gets us our results in the Leaving Certificate. Not only do we ignore the first and second part of the brain, but we focus our attention almost exclusively on only one half of the third part of the brain. We have, by now, become used to the distinction made by neuropsychologists between the left hemisphere of the brain and the right or 'minor' hemisphere which 'was presumed, usually contemptuously, to be more "primitive" than the left, the latter being seen as the unique flower of human evolution'.

> And in a sense this is correct: the left hemisphere is more sophisticated and specialised, a very late outgrowth of the primate, and especially hominid, brain. On the other hand, it is the right hemisphere which controls the crucial powers of recognising reality which every living creature must have in order to survive. The left hemisphere, like a computer tacked onto the basic creatural brain, is designed for programs and schematics; and classical neurology was more concerned with schematics than with reality, so that when, at last, some of the right-hemisphere syndromes emerged, they were considered bizarre.[81]

Writing in 1985, Oliver Sacks suggested that 'the entire history of neurology and neuropsychology can be seen as a history of the investigation of the left hemisphere'.[82]

Mythic intelligence is an essential kind of human understanding and it is to our great impoverishment that

---

[81] Oliver Sacks, *The Man Who Mistook His Wife For a Hat* (London: Duckworth, 1985), p. 2
[82] Ibid.

our educational systems and our academic leaders treat it with such contempt. Ernst Cassirer's *The Philosophy of Symbolic Forms* explains how 'the mythical intuition of space' occupies 'a kind of middle position between the space of sense perception and the space of pure cognition, that is, geometry'.[83] In other words, the mythic is the way of viewing the world through the limbic system. The space of perception, which is the space of vision, of touch, of smell, of taste, of hearing, is not the same as the space of pure mathematics, which is the world of the neocortex; 'there is indeed a thoroughgoing divergence between the two'. 'In contrast to the homogeneity which prevails in the conceptual space of geometry every position and direction in mythical space is endowed as it were with a particular accent.'[84] And this form of consciousness, this kind of knowledge, has every right to exist, to be cultivated, promoted, and valorised, just as much as the mathematical and geometrical. So it is not a question of denying the value of mathematical and scientific knowledge. It is rather a question of reinstating another kind of knowledge which is equally important and *sui generis*.

In a review by Robert Graves of a book by Dr Anne Ross, *Pagan Celtic Britain*, Graves believes that this highly qualified academic celtologist is barred from understanding the very material she is writing about because of her scientific education.[85] 'As a girl of seventeen Dr Ross had done what anthropologists call "field-work" by learning Gaelic for six months in a West Highland peasant's hut. Then after graduating at Edinburgh, she took an educational job in the same Goidelic region, but later returned to Edinburgh for a

---

[83] Ernst Cassirer, *The Philosophy of Symbolic Forms* (Yale: Yale University Press, 1955). Vol. I, 'Language'; Vol. II, 'Mythical Thought'; Vol. III, 'The Phenomenology of Knowledge'; Vol. IV, 'The Metaphysics of Symbolic Forms'.

[84] Ibid., Vol. II, pp. 83–5.

[85] Robert Graves, *The Crane Bag and Other Disputed Subjects* (London: Cassell, 1969), pp. 1–9.

degree in Celtic studies and a Ph.D. in Celtic archaeology.'
Thus, according to Graves, 'she forgot ... how to think in
Gaelic Crofter style, which means poetically.' He makes his
point by quoting her treatment of an important Celtic myth
about the 'crane bag' of the sea-god Manannán Mac Lir. This
bag had been made for the Sea God from the skin of a
woman magically transformed into a crane:

> This crane bag held every precious thing that
> Manannán possessed. The shirt of Manannán himself
> and his knife, and the shoulder-strap of Goibne, the
> fierce smith, together with his smith's hook; also the
> king of Scotland's shears; and the King of Lochlainn's
> helmet; and the bones of Asil's swine. A strip of the
> great whale's back was also in that shapely crane bag.
> When the sea was full, all the treasures were visible
> in it; when the fierce sea ebbed, the crane bag was
> empty.

Dr Ross is like the rest of us: trained out of poetic sensibility.
She has lost the art of reading the signs of the times.
According to Graves, she 'can make nothing of such fairy-
tale material'. He has to interpret for her:

> What the fabulous crane bag contained was
> alphabetical secrets known only to oracular priests
> and poets. The inspiration came, it is said, from
> observing a flock of cranes, 'which make letters as
> they fly'. The letters are formed against the sky by the
> wings, legs, beaks and heads of these shapely birds.
> Hermes, messenger to the Gods, afterwards reduced
> these shapes to written characters. Cranes were in fact
> totem birds of the poetically educated priests ... That
> the Crane Bag filled when the sea was in flood, but
> emptied when it ebbed, means that these Ogham
> signs made complete sense for the poetic sons of
> Manannán, but none for uninitiated outsiders. The

crane bag was not, in fact, a tangible object, but existed only as a metaphor.

Dr Ross, as an academic archeologist, has the job of digging up 'things' from the past, dating and comparing them. But as a trained scientist, 'she can accept no poetic or religious magic'. Anything that falls outside the scope of her 'academic conditioning' is 'branded as mythical – mythical being, like Pagan, a word that denies truth to any ancient non-Christian emblem, metaphor or poetic anecdote'. We too have been overly trained in scientific prejudices. We no longer see the world as symbol.

W. B. Yeats's intelligence was essentially mythic. Such intelligence weaves its way through symbols and has a very different perspective on the universe to that of the scientist, for instance.

> I wished for a world where I could discover this tradition perpetually, and not in pictures and in poems only, but in tiles round the chimney-piece and in the hangings that kept out the draught. I had even created a dogma: 'Because those imaginary people are created out of the deepest instinct of man, to be his measure and his norm, whatever I can imagine those mouths speaking may be the nearest I can go to truth'. When I listened they seemed always to speak of one thing only: they, their loves, every incident of their lives, were steeped in the supernatural.[86]

Even to understand this last quotation we have to reintroduce ourselves to a mythic way of thinking.

In Western European philosophy we were introduced by Auguste Comte to the idea that human intelligence had

---

[86] W. B. Yeats, *Four Years 1887–1891* (Dublin: The Cuala Press, 1921), pp. 4–5. Published in *Autobiographies* (London: Macmillan, 1955), pp. 115–16.

developed from a primitive mythic stage, through a medieval metaphysical stage, right up to the scientific rationalism which has so marked and transformed our world. This development was linear and rendered all stages that preceded it obsolete. There is no such evolutionary progress in a linear model, which casts off the previous in an advance towards the present, as a rocket might detach itself from the parts that launch it. Mythic intelligence is an essential kind of human understanding and it is to our great impoverishment that our educational systems and our academic leaders treat it with such contempt.

It is difficult for us to step outside the spaceship and recognise just how programmed we are. In much the same way that we recognise the overwhelming extent to which we are dependent upon electricity only when there is a power cut, we have to exercise our imagination almost violently to recognise the extent to which we are automised clones of an infrastructural grid maintained with devastating tenacity by the guardians of academic protocol. In our schools we must make room for all aspects of our tripartite brain as well as all functions of our lives as human beings. This is not as easy as it sounds because we have to recognise the extent to which we have been cauterised and paralysed by a long history of concentration on one aspect and total neglect of all the others. If you don't use it you lose it, and we have lost the capacity to think mythically and to encounter the world around us other than through the microscope or the telescope of our highly intelligent but restricted neocortical surface areas.

CHAPTER SEVEN

Music in Numbers

If light, warmth, power, enjoyment and comfort are our primordial dreams, then modern research is science, permeated by the hard, courageous, mobile, knife-cold, knife-sharp mode of thought that is mathematics. We have gained in terms of reality and lost in terms of the dream. We no longer lie under a tree gazing up at the sky between our big toe and second toe; we are too busy getting on with our jobs. And it is no good being lost in dreams and going hungry, if one wants to be efficient; one must eat steak and get a move on. It is exactly as if that old-time, inefficient mankind had gone to sleep on an ant-hill, and when the new one woke up the ants had crept into its blood; and ever since then it has had to fling itself about with the greatest of violence, without ever being able to shake off this beastly sensation of ant-like industry ... Mathematics has entered like a daemon into all aspects of our life ... maybe we no longer believe in a Devil to whom we can sell our soul ... but all those who know something of the soul bear witness to the fact that it has been ruined by mathematics and that in mathematics is the source of a wicked intellect that, while making us lord of the earth has also made us slaves of the machine.[87]

Let me quote from 'Better Literacy and Numeracy for Children and Young People: A Draft National Plan to Improve Literacy and Numeracy in Schools', issued by the Department of Education in November 2010:

---

[87] Robert Musil, *The Man Without Qualities*, Vol. I (Milwaukee: Panther Books, 1968), p. 74.

In recent years there have been demands from organisations, interest groups and various educators that additional emphasis should be placed in school curricula on such areas as social and life skills, environmental issues, arts and music education ... among others. While curricula have been adjusted in the light of some of these concerns, we have to recognise that the curricula cannot mediate all issues that are of relevance to young people. Including a broader range of issues, topics and subjects in school curricula inevitably has meant that the time available for the acquisition and consolidation of critical core skills has been eroded.

For critical core skills here read 'literacy and numeracy', not human communication and dialogue.

Here again we have to take a longer look at this emphasis on literacy and numeracy. Civilised societies of the twentieth century democratised the languages of reading, writing and arithmetic. These became the fundamental currency in the West. They also became the criteria for 'intelligence', as those who have fallen between the bars of the grid know too well when they become marginalised and deprived by illiteracy. We imagine that reading and writing are natural to us, whereas, in fact, they must be two of the most unnatural activities ever undertaken.

Walter Ong has examined the history of our versatility in these areas. He shows how a language such as high Latin which was never a 'mother tongue' (taught by one's mother) to later generations of Europeans became their only access to so-called higher education. Obviously Latin was once a spoken language but it became a 'school language', completely controlled by writing, once it ceased to be a vernacular tongue for those who used it.

For well over a thousand years, Latin was a language written and spoken by males for the most part. It was nobody's mother tongue and was learnt outside the home as a foreign language. It had no direct connection with the unconscious, as any vernacular learnt from early childhood would have. There was no baby talk associated with it and it was taught with all the punitive hardships and rigorous academic settings that were the hallmarks of our schools. It was a first language to none of its users, and since each of them spoke it with an accent peculiar to their particular country, none of them could understand it as spoken by the other. This meant that it became essentially a written language because it was always recorded in the same way and could be understood as a written text by all who had learnt it. This 'learned Latin' became a striking example of how the power of writing first of all isolates discourse. It has to be translated into an objective form before it can become part of a dialogue. But this very isolation was also the cause of an unparalleled productivity, which was the result of such concentrated solitude. This strange phenomenon made possible 'the exquisitely abstract world of medieval scholasticism', which in turn created 'the new mathematical modern science which followed on the scholastic experience'. Ong suggests that without learned Latin as an abstract written language cut off from the psychic roots of our normal vernacular languages, 'modern science would have got underway with greater difficulty, if it had got underway at all'. Our kind of literacy and numeracy is rooted in the abstract written language which was the *lingua franca* of all the universities of Europe for a thousand years. 'Modern science grew in Latin soil,' according to Ong, 'for philosophers and scientists through the time of Sir Isaac Newton commonly both wrote and did their abstract thinking in Latin.'[88]

We are all victims or beneficiaries of this legacy depending on how you wish to view it. The results are spectacular in one way and can be proved immediately.

---

[88] Walter J. Ong, *Orality and Literacy, The Technologizing of the Word* (London & New York: Routledge, 1982); the edition I quote from is 2000, pp. 113–4.

What is happening at this moment for you, as a reader, is a case in point. Between you and me, at this moment in your life, is a page of print. These words form a code, which, because you can read and I can write, allow me to communicate with you. The process is similar to drip-feeding. A vast multitude crowds towards one tiny entrance where one word appears at a time. I can only write one word at a time. I fill this page slowly and separately so that I can tell you word for word what is on my mind. You have become so used to gobbling up these units that you may not even notice the cumbersome technique necessary for you to eventually land these ideas in your mind. So, we have to ask ourselves whether we may not have lost almost as much as we have gained from our much vaunted literacy and numeracy skills, and, if so, we must see to it that our children have the very best of both worlds.

Of course there is an advantage to having a common language. The language of scientific formulae is an invariant and universal expression. Other languages are relative. If I say 'John is here now', my meaning depends on who John is, on where I am, and on when I happen to be speaking. The sentence could be referring to John the Baptist, John of Gaunt, or Pope John XXIII. In which case the word 'here' could refer to Palestine, England or Italy, and 'now' relate to the first century BCE, the fourteenth or the twentieth centuries. In science no such flexibility, wooliness, or ambiguity is allowed.

The trouble is that education of intelligence has also become standardised and only one variety has been valorised. Anything apart from the standard IQ has to fend for itself. Reading was, up to now, the standard way of sending information around the world. The new language of computerised technology may change this monocultural bias in the twenty-first century and impose a less demanding and more accessible common currency. However, for the present this ability remains essential. Without it we are unable to cope in the world we have created.

The development of the three Rs as the standard syllabus for all primary education displaced our capacity to see life as a mystery and prepared us to face it as a problem to be solved. The second set of cyphers to be learned was not as easy or as communicable as the first. Numeracy was not as widespread as literacy. Only certain minorities became expert and conversant.

People had to learn to read and write the language of measurement, if they were to understand modern science. This meant a no-nonsense approach to numbers, depriving them of their magic. In the beginning we grunted and extemporised verbally when trying to do our sums on the turnips or the cattle we were counting or bartering.

Our fingers are visual aids to counting. In its initial stages, number was more of a manual than an intellectual concept. The Latin word for a finger is *digitus*, from which our term 'digit' and its adjective, 'digital', derive. The fact that we have five fingers on each hand, allowing us with natural ease to count up to ten, introduces another familiar term: the Latin word for ten, *decimus*, which introduces us to the decimal system. It was the Arabs who invented this 'handy' system for counting, which took ten as its base. If I had ten objects to account for I could cope. In at least one ancient language the word for 'six' is equivalent to the word for 'jump', reminding our ancestors that after five they were required to jump over to the other hand to continue the process of calculation. In Euclidean geometry (the word 'geometry' means 'measurement of the world') the assumptions are explicit: the premises and conclusions derived from them are formulated in words. Mathematics, which, as we surmised, originated as a most natural way of counting, using our hands and sometimes our feet, had to undergo an excision of verbal content to attain symbolic exactness. 5+5 = 10 is an exercise most of us can manage, as shorthand for the ten fingers on both our hands. However, five times that number is more complicated and requires a kind of juggling. Thus it was later replaced with an easier, more manageable symbol, 'X', which became the sign or symbol for multiplication, so that 5 x 5 = 5+5+5+5+5. We are still within reach of our hands and our feet: digital calculation.

But in Algebra (in Arabic the word *jabara* means 'reunite'), the ties between words and operations and between objects and symbols are cut so that the operations and symbols can be brought into closer mutual conformity. It is a language, but not connected to 'the real world', and it is therefore restricted to defining relationships between signs and symbols. It is a language that takes place in our heads. As the activity becomes more abstract and sophisticated it is removed from the tangible world where most of us can find our feet, so to speak. We all know those people who have a gift for mathematics and those others who can't handle it at all. We're into a more rarefied world not accessible to everyone, as the symbolism of reading and writing are supposed to be.

However, as mathematicians move further and further into rarefied abstraction, we leave behind an understanding of and sensibility towards numbers, which is now regarded as primitive and obsolete. Numbers for our ancestors were keys to the secrets of the universe. Astrology supplied the belief that all aggregates with the same number were related: four seasons, four elements, four points of the compass, for instance; seven days in a week, seven planets. This was why there were seven sacraments, seven virtues, seven deadly sins, and so on. Such arithmetico-mystical attitudes to numbers have vanished, apart from various childish jingles and abiding superstitions which remind us of their former stronghold. Perfectly rational people refuse to take room number 13 in a hotel – indeed, some hotels refuse to have a room of that number. And the way we teach children to count magpies is revealing:

1 for sorrow
2 for joy
3 for a girl

4 for a boy
5 for silver
6 for gold
7 for a secret never to be told.

The nursery rhyme, as often, contains far more than it pretends and the number seven is representative of some hidden wisdom which helps us to understand the world we live in. There is no necessity to develop further the arithmetico-mystical tradition that inspired our forefathers, from Pythagoras who said 'everything is number', right through the whole of the Middle Ages.[89] Our present, very restricted and univocal interpretation of numbers is not more than three centuries old and is not shared by other cultures. The purpose of these reminders is to sensitise readers to another way of looking at numbers which is not to be discounted.

The problem with our inherited world is not the hierarchy of different symbolic systems available to us to enjoy the spectrum of experience which spans the radar screen of human consciousness; it is, rather, the dearth of such systems when it comes to neglected areas, especially those which are unconscious. We have only to think of the language of emotion to find an area where education and trained sensibility are in short supply. Each person is left to fend for themselves in one of the most poignant and inescapable areas of our experience. And yet it seems obvious that each of us should be given at least the rudiments of one of the most elusive and important symbolic systems if we are even to begin to understand human relationships. This would require tapping into a wavelength and a communications system other than the cerebral, reaching what has been called the 'sympathetic

---

[89] Vincent Foster Hopper, *Medieval Number Symbolism, Its Sources, Meaning, and Influence on Thought and Expression* (New York: Columbia University Press, 1938), p. 33.

system' as opposed to the cerebro-spinal one which covers the three Rs of traditional education.

There is a language of symbols which can help us to grapple with the unconscious. The middle ages were fluent in such dialect. The world was a multilayered tableau of symbols. As above, so below; as in the foreground so in the background. There was a correspondence between everything in heaven and on earth and the medieval mind was attuned to the connections which should and could be made. Hidden signs and symbols connected the phenomenal universe. These revealed themselves in similar qualities and associations, whether audible or visible: colour and shape, volume and weight, texture and movement, these could be compared and aligned just as sounds if similar could unveil a code of correspondence.

It is important to recognise that for many years this other kind of knowledge has been undermined if not suppressed. From four years of age, children are condemned to a bookish, commercial education. Recent decisions of the United Nations propose to inflict this myopia on all children of the world in the name of equality of educational opportunity and universal human rights. Of course it is a very good thing that everyone on the planet should be able to read, write and do arithmetic; the impoverishment occurs when we think that this is all they need to be taught to do. If we are really to be educated as human beings we have to be in touch with our inner snake.

Most of our education from the age of four is at a third remove from the reality we perceive around us. Between the metric space of mathematics and physics and the topological space of our childhood world there are several symbolic variations to which we have access as children and which we ignore and abandon to our cost. Children are naturally in touch with all parts of their brains, the limbic and the serpentine as well as the neocortex. Such capabilities are erased by the age of eighteen. This can be called colonisation by the neocortex.

Music, art and myth are symbolic systems or structures which allow us to process the subtle way in which the world attaches itself to the delicate sprockets of our sensibility and psyche. This makes it hugely important, for our eventual integration, to maintain these channels, these connections with our triune brain, because mathematics and physics by the nature of their operative efficacy are obliged to dissociate completely from the subjective world of feeling. The facts of physics are not on the same footing with the facts of history because they rest on entirely different presuppositions and intellectual procedures. They work from another portion of the brain. We take three important steps towards this third remove from reality, and each step is a different part of the brain's functioning. Education that neglects these intermediary symbolic stages between the world of sensation and the world of the three Rs is unbalanced.

Unless we bring all three parts of the brain into dialogue with each other, dysfunction sets in. Many of my generation grew up on Edgar Rice Burroughs' stories of *Tarzan of the Apes*. These stories give us a graphic description of the separation between the serpentine brain and the neocortex. By placing Tarzan in the jungle among the apes, the writer positions us geographically and sociologically in the atavistic and primeval atmosphere where our serpentine brains emerge. The sudden transfer to Lord Greystoke's aristocratic home in England betokens the more sophisticated and later appearance of the neocortex as the third brain which evolved and covered over its more primitive ancestor. We live constantly in the tensions between the two. Tarzan, brought up in the jungle by gorillas, discovers that he is really Lord Greystoke, and when he comes home to afternoon tea with cucumber sandwiches and a game of croquet on the lawn, he is apt suddenly to tear off all his clothes and 'go ape' when one of the guests steals the silver or stains the carpet.

Our serpentine brain is deeply connected to our sense of smell. For illiterate cultures, the sense of smell was paramount and there was a huge contribution from it to all social interaction. Sexual attraction has always been strongly associated with scent. An average perfume, I am told, has over 300 ingredients. Wherever we are, we are surrounded by at least half a million smells. Each of us is equipped with that unobtrusive and often cheekily attractive piece of equipment commonly referred to as the nose, basically a tube or a colander with about 5 million sniffer cells on either side. Our civilisation has done its best to anaesthetise this faculty. We have become obsessed with obliterating it with deodorants and air fresheners and all manner of masking agents.

So much for the bad smells, but what about the good ones? When describing a particular scent that we enjoy, we move to the neocortex and try to create an image in a smell space. We might describe a perfume as 'peachy apricot', for example. The higher echelons of the perfume world treat us to a whole scale of values in terms of musical notation, where the rose is your middle C, the top notes are the first impressions you get, lasting for no more than a few minutes, the middle notes are those that waft around you for about half an hour, and the bass notes are the ones that remain throughout the day.

In the disturbing and occasionally repulsive novel *Perfume: The Story of a Murderer,* first published in 1985, Patrick Süskind explores the idea that our ability to smell – and the ability of others to smell us – is essential to our humanity. The most gifted human nose recognises about 10,000 scents. Jean-Baptiste Grenouille, the main character in *Perfume*, has just such a nose. Grenouille can recall every odour he has ever encountered; he smells a worm in an apple, money hidden behind a brick wall, and people walking several blocks away. He develops a plan to rule the world: 'people could close their eyes to greatness, to horrors, to beauty, and their ears to melodies or deceiving words. But they could not escape scent. For scent was a brother of breath ... He who ruled scent ruled the hearts of men.'[90]

---

[90] Patrick Süskind, *Perfume: The Story of a Murderer* (London: Penguin, 2010), p. 161.

There are three parts to our triune brain and unless our systems of education accept this fact and provide adequate and appropriate training and attention to all three, they are failing to educate the whole person. At present it would seem that the neocortex is the only part of our brain provided for. The limbic brain, which works mythically and poetically, is treated as a poor relation, whereas the serpentine brain, which articulates our instinctive selves, is mostly left to its own devices without any recognition or organised programme in the curriculum.

When we claim that education is essentially a personal relationship, this means that the person of the teacher is the mediator between every one of us and our genuine personhood. Just as we have to enter this world through the human body of another person, so this confusing world has to be mediated to us by a human person. Education is being led out into the world by a teacher who has learnt how to make this connection. The teacher is a human person with enough imagination and humility to know which parts of this wonderful world are likely to open the door for us into our own personhood. Becoming a person means entering that space between us and the world around us. Education means nothing less than creative encounter with the precise person who can unlock that door.

On 3 March 1887, Anne Sullivan arrived in Tuscumbia, Alabama, and for the first time met Helen Keller – blind, deaf and dumb from her birth. Anne and Helen moved into a small cottage on the land of the main house. After a month of Anne's teaching, there occurred what the people of the time called a 'miracle'. Anne had started teaching Helen to finger spell. Although Helen could repeat these finger movements she could not understand what they meant. When Anne led her to the water pump on 5 April 1887, all that was about to change. As Anne pumped the water over Helen's hand, Anne spelled out the word 'water' in the girl's free hand. Something about this explained the meaning of words within Helen, and Anne could immediately see in her face that she finally understood. Helen later recounted the incident:

> We walked down the path to the well-house, attracted by the fragrance of the honey-suckle with which it was covered. Someone was drawing water and my teacher placed my hand under the spout. As the cool stream gushed over one hand she spelled into the other the word 'water', first slowly, then rapidly. I stood still, my whole attention fixed upon the motions of her fingers. Suddenly I felt a misty consciousness as of something forgotten, a thrill of returning thought, and somehow the mystery of language was revealed to me.[91]

There are three vitally important things here: the place where it happened, the inspired teacher and the capacity to see in the face of the child that she has understood. It is that electric moment that every teacher should be looking for. This means that the learning process must begin with an awareness of a personal centre of significant living, the place in every child where understanding can begin. From such a place all experience becomes meaningful. Like Helen Keller, each one of us is blind, deaf and dumb to the real significance of the world we enter, and we await the revelation of the mystery of the world's language through the inspirational guidance of a gifted educator.

---

[91] Helen Keller, *The Story of My Life* (1903; New York: Cosimo Inc., 2010), p. 12.

CHAPTER EIGHT

Alexander Pushkin in Ireland

Before he went to school
he could read the bark of trees,
leaf veins,
seashell-convolutions,
footprints,
and the touch of fingers;
now he goes to school,
and he can only read words.

Jennifer Farley

There have always been teachers who have attempted to provide structured and sustained training for the neglected limbic brain in a way that is accessible to every child, but these are the exceptionally gifted ones who are few and far between. Children should not have to wait until they have the good fortune to happen upon one such teacher during their lives at school. The large number of artists and poets in the country, many of whom admit that they either failed to make the grade within, or that they fell out of, the official educational system, is witness to the natural talent and ubiquitous raw material ever present in every child. But for most of us the limbic brain has been left fallow. No one is denying the rights and the abilities of the neocortex, nor the excellent system which has been put in place to promote and develop this. However, if there is no effort to ensure that the other two levels of our brains are allowed to keep pace, then our education system is unbalanced and can only produce people who are similarly unbalanced. The Pushkin movement in Ireland is one tiny attempt to promote imagination in the education system as it stands.

What came to be known as the Pushkin movement began with the cry of a child, the first child of the Duke and Duchess of Abercorn, born in Northern Ireland in the late 1960s. Every child in the province must have registered an atmosphere of psychic invasion. The Pushkin movement was initiated as creative counterpoint to such destructive forces polluting the lives of children.

Sacha Duchess of Abercorn has roots on her maternal side in Russia. Both Tsar Nicholas I and Alexander Pushkin, the poet, were her ancestors. She married James, Duke of Abercorn in 1966 and came to live in Northern Ireland when she was twenty years of age. 'Shortly after it became my home, however,' she said in an interview, 'Northern Ireland – which had seemed, on the surface at least, a serenely beautiful and peaceful place – descended into thirty years of sectarian warfare. Despair and mistrust contaminated the very air we breathed.'

In 1986, the 150th anniversary of Pushkin's death, Luton Hoo, her grandmother's home in England, became the venue for a weekend of events to commemorate the life and works of Russia's greatest poet. People from diverse backgrounds and ideologies – representatives of the Soviet regime of the time, as well as émigrés who had fled the Revolution, their children and grandchildren – were united for a brief weekend by the beauty of Pushkin's words. Russians who had previously regarded each other as enemies found common ground. In the course of that brief meeting, poetry and music achieved what seventy years of diplomacy had failed to achieve. 'Thanks in large part to my grandmother, I grew up with an awareness of how profoundly Pushkin's poetic voice was loved by his countrymen. When I came to Ireland I found myself in another land where the poetic voice enjoyed a similarly powerful resonance. It struck me that just as Pushkin had brought Russians of different factions together, so he – or his spirit – might kindle a similar spark in Ireland. I wondered whether it might be possible, under his guiding spirit, to bring together children from different traditions in Ireland, from North and South, from urban and rural schools. I wondered if it might thereby become possible to help them to express their thoughts and feelings, their inner lives, by creative means.'[92]

A green light was given in 1987 to launch a pilot programme with schools in Donegal and Tyrone. Nobel laureate Seamus Heaney and poet Michael Longley agreed to act as co-patrons. The Pushkin Prizes began with just eight schools – four Catholic and four Protestant. Since then, the movement has spread across the whole island of Ireland. More than 50,000 children have participated. Imagination has brought them together in ways that traditional educational structures had not. It has helped to break down at least some of the barriers and encouraged the development of friendships.

Helen Cannon, a primary school teacher, first experienced the Pushkin programme as a practitioner in the classroom for three years, and then, because she was so convinced of its importance, applied for the job of co-ordinator of the programme itself. From 1999 to 2002 she left her job as a national school teacher in Clare to become education director of the Pushkin project. She called this her 'escape to reality'. Helen recognised that 'nothing captured the imagination of [her] students like the Pushkin project'. She went on to write her Ph.D. thesis on the creation and the effect of this movement in the various schools and on the different pupils who participated.[93]

---

[92] Speech given by the Duchess of Abercorn on the reception of the Princess Grace Humanitarian Award in Monaco (8 October 2006). www.irelandfunds.org/pdf/pushkin_trust_10fw.pdf.

[93] Helen Cannon, *Promoting 'Lifetime Writers' in Primary Classrooms: An Analysis of the Pushkin Model, 1999–2002*, Ph.D. thesis, University College Dublin, 2006.

For fifteen years a creative writing competition was the centre of the Pushkin schools' programme, in which fifty schools from both Northern Ireland and the Republic of Ireland participated each year. In 2002–2003 the creative writing competition evolved into a cross-curricular awards programme. This initiative still retained creative writing as a central core activity but this was supplemented in participating schools by other creative art forms. Now, after twenty-five years of practical experience, a methodology has been developed and has proved both its coinage and its credibility.

It is not incidental to the success of this experiment that it took place in one of the most beautiful settings in the Irish countryside. The 1,500-acre Baronscourt estate in Co. Tyrone, situated in a sheltered valley in the foothills of the Sperrin mountains, is among a handful of old family estates which have survived intact and which combine historical and architectural interest with a landscape of natural beauty. Each generation of the Abercorn family, who have lived there since 1610, has continued to enhance the splendour of the estate with constant planting and landscaping of the park and gardens. Anyone visiting the estate is struck by the magnificent vistas and spectacular walks, embellished every season by the particular beauty of the time of year. The stark tracery of winter trees stretched out like sheet music for the spring and summer are enhanced in those seasons by displays of masses of bluebells, rhododendrons and azaleas. Carefully tended woods frame cultivated views across lakes and valleys. This is an enchanted island where children are immediately connected with the beauty of nature. That it should be made available as an educational experience is an incalculable resource for the children of our future and hopefully it sets an inspiring example for comparable estates throughout the island.

As a focus for and dedication to the work of imagination on the Baronscourt estate, the duchess has had built a wooden *dacha* where all such work for children receives its inspiration. This centre is called Pushkin House. Teachers, artists and environmentalists with a common interest in education come together here on a regular basis to promote the cause of such holistic experience. Methodologies develop out of their interchange of ideas and shared learning experience. No one holds the key in these circumstances, although each has something to contribute. The eventual pattern emerges from what works and what doesn't. This requires an experiential approach to the creative arts, placing greater emphasis on the process rather than the product, in the belief that actual firsthand experience is more worthwhile than the eventual emergence of a work. All those taking part enjoy a positive, enthusiastic ambiance in which to carry out their creative endeavours, which, in turn, stimulates and promotes quality work.

Teachers who have taken part in these workshops find that they exercise a long-term impact on their own way of teaching, and say that they are not the same kind of teacher afterwards. The actual experience of creativity releases a hidden reality which gives them confidence and allows them to be more relaxed and surefooted when engaging with the originality of a younger generation. Without such personal liberation they can find themselves fearful and negative when creativity in the classroom is at full flow.

Even more transformative are workshops facilitated by artists and environmentalists, where children, teachers and parents are equal partners. Such shared endeavour removes the hierarchical overtones and restrictive parameters of inherited school structures. Finally, celebrating the achievements of such self-expression by a publication or performance, without introducing competitive or judgemental attitudes, provides a recognisable marker and enhances the experience.[94]

For the past twenty-five years, the Pushkin Trust has been bringing together schoolchildren from both sides of the border to nurture their creativity. Writers, dancers, musicians and artists work with the children during one-day

---

[94] Ibid., p. 337.

workshops and extended summer camps of the imagination. It's all free, sponsored by donations and grants, with a modest annual turnover for the Trust of around £250,000. The annual creative-writing competition has been judged by such writers as Doris Lessing, Roald Dahl and John Banville, among others. The late Ted Hughes, a long-time friend of the duchess, was involved in the early years.

This year, 2012, at the Grand Opera House in Belfast, there was a celebration of twenty-five years of 'The Spirit of Pushkin in Ireland' featuring Katie Melua, who composed a song especially for the event. She sang this song, 'The Story's Magic', with children from all over the country who have been connected with the Pushkin movement. They were also joined by the Pushkin Performers, many of whom are children from schools both sides of the border. Seamus Heaney, a patron of the Trust from the beginning, sent the following message for the occasion: 'The message emanating from the Pushkin Trust ... is a message in praise of creative joy and psychic integrity, of trust in potential and impatience with cliché, a call to everybody to be more ardently and originally themselves.'

Educators from all over Ireland have paid tribute to the ability of Pushkin to inspire. Teachers and pupils have described how their contact with this movement helped to unlock in them a creative potential they never knew existed. Such hidden treasure inside themselves might always have lain dormant in their normal school lives but was triggered into life and has never left them since. They attribute this life-changing experience to a specific occasion when the magic of Pushkin worked for them.

Obviously, such talk of 'magic' is dangerous. It seems to describe some quick-fix programme that provides children with powers that are otherwise inaccessible. The truth is more simple. So much has to happen before and after any such educational success story can happen. But it is experienced by those to whom it happens as an instantaneous occurrence. It takes longer to ensure that the initial experience is cultivated and that it endures. But the process may begin over a few days. For maximum impact and long-term effect it takes time to develop. There has to be the possibility to tap back into the source of inspiration again and again. Every child has a wealth of imagination which comes naturally and is expressed in games and behaviour patterns usually ignored by the adult world. The systems of education which we have inherited, and to which most of our children are exposed systematically, stifle all such playful virtuosity. The answer to the question of how we should promote imagination in our children is so simple that it can be overlooked. We don't have to do anything, it is already there – it only has to be allowed to flourish. We don't have to promote it, we only have to remove the obstacles we have put in its way and allow it time and the ambiance conducive to its display of itself. Providing the atmosphere and the channel for imagination is the magic of Pushkin.

The Shankill road (*Seanchill* means 'old church' in Irish) is the arterial road leading through west Belfast. It is lined by shops and runs through the predominantly Loyalist working-class area of the city. The residents live in the many streets which branch off the main road. The district is located between the Falls Road at one end and Ardoyne at the other. The Falls Road is synonymous with the Republican communities in the city. Ardoyne is also an Irish Nationalist working-class and mainly Catholic district. During 'the Troubles' the Greater Shankill and its residents were subjected to a number of bombings and shootings by Irish republican paramilitary forces. It then became a centre for loyalist paramilitarism. The Ulster Volunteer Force (UVF) had its genesis there as early as 1966, and the Ulster Defence Association (UDA) was established there in September 1971, when some vigilante groups merged into this larger structure. The 'Shankill Butchers' is the name given to an Ulster Loyalist gang, many of whom were members of the UVF who conducted paramilitary activities in the 1970s in Belfast, killing at least thirty people (including a significant number of Protestants) in sectarian attacks, paramilitary feuds, bombing raids and personal grudges.

Despite extensive police resources channelled towards their capture, a wall of silence created by a mixture of fear and respect in the Shankill community provided few leads that could be followed. As the district is located between the Falls Road at one end and Ardoyne at the other, local residents (as well as their nationalist neighbours) found themselves unwilling targets for crossfire as both sets of paramilitaries attacked each other and each other's communities.

Children in this area were traumatised by the violence and the breakdown of normal life in society so that many were unable to follow the normal curriculum at school. The Pushkin Trust had an enormous influence on the curriculum in all schools in the Shankill area for one full academic year. All the primary schools (state and church), the two secondary schools, and the parents of the children worked on the Pushkin theme, 'The Fire Within', for almost three full terms before putting on a highly professional programme, which they performed in the Waterfront Hall in Belfast on 31 May 2007 to an audience of 2,000 people from all over Northern Ireland. The schools had Pushkin facilitators working on various aspects of the creative arts.

Betty Orr MBE has been principal of Edenbrooke Primary School on Tennent Street since 1993. She is also on the board of the Pushkin Trust. She introduced the 'enriched curriculum'[95] for the children who were too distressed to cope with the academic programme. Then she arranged for several of the children to go to Baronscourt and follow the

---

[95] The Enriched Curriculum is a primary school education program which started in Northern Ireland as a pilot scheme in the year 2000, as it was obvious that the old teaching methods were not meeting the needs of young people. based on learning through structured play so that the child can enjoy their learning experience and therefore will want to learn.

Pushkin programme. The children were so enthusiastic about this and benefitted so greatly that they asked if they could bring their mothers with them the next time. There were about twenty children and the next time they came there were about ten mothers with them. The children began teaching their mothers, showing them around the estate and telling them what they had learned previously.

Adrian Rice, a writer, arranged some programmes for these parents and persuaded them to write down their experiences. They were extremely reluctant at first, but when he had the idea that they should tell the story of the Shankill Road as if the road itself were telling the story, they sparked into life. He made a little book of this voice for the Shankill Road and put it online.

And this 'magic' has now been practised so often and has achieved such startling success, especially with students who were regarded as underachievers in their own school environment, that the organisers have been able to analyse the process and describe in slow-motion how it happens. Its effect is palpable after the experience, not just with children but more importantly with teachers and parents who sometimes accompanied their children and were reluctantly dragged into the magic circle, even though they had intended to remain outside observers. Essential to the Pushkin experience is the joy of discovering the unique imprint which we can all make, that no one else can make no matter how faltering or inadequate that contribution may objectively prove to be. It is the taking of these initial steps, however fumbling or ungainly, that opens the sluice gates to further imaginative endeavour. These tentative steps and the ensuing confidence that they bring are the essential permission we need to further explore our imaginative capacities. And this confidence spills over into all other aspects of our lives and our work.

All that is required for such a 'Pushkin' experience is to arrive in a beautiful natural setting like Baronscourt, although it could also be in any other beautiful place around the country. There you will meet others who are gathered for the same purpose, and it doesn't matter their age, their race, their creed, their background. A knowledgeable environmentalist who is also a gifted communicator leads the group around the woods and lakes and points out things happening in nature that we might not notice if we were on our own. The participants are encouraged to collect some of the items of nature that seem to call to them, stones, branches, leaves, feathers, flowers, whatever takes their fancy. Then the group returns to a room or a designated area where they can describe or express whatever it is they have experienced in nature on their walk using some art form, whether it be music, sculpture, poetry, drama or painting. At the end there is a presentation of the various art pieces to the others or to those who come to collect each participant at the end of the day, or of the session, if it lasts for longer than a day. It is always more powerful to stay over in the chosen place so that dreams and visitations in the night can be included in the artwork the next day. Such engagement with nature and release of artistic impulse cannot be described at second hand – it has to be experienced personally. It occurs like a revolution in one's life; it touches and unleashes energies which had never before been recognised. Most people who have a Pushkin experience at Baronscourt name it as one of the turning points in their lives.

The three moments of the original Baronscourt experience come together inside the person as an illumination, as a light going on, in a way that is made absolute by a never-again-to-be-denied personal experience. From this moment onwards I begin to live and to act out of a self-evident principle, which I didn't read in books or learn from any other person, but which I personally experienced in the depths of my own heart as an original impulse and which I can never again deny.

Teachers who have done the programme for 'inspirational teaching' say they will never again teach in the way they used to.[96] This does not mean that it produces some mercurial wizardry which strikes like lightning to affect us either personally or professionally. The programme does have an immediate and palpable effect but it also provides a necessary and sustained support system which follows through over a lengthy period to ensure perseverance and long-term durability of the initial breakthrough. However, this should not undersell or detract from the 'magic' which initiates the whole process. Each individual person has to experience the unlocking of their own imaginative capacity as an absolute reality.

The tripartite experience effects an interior transformation, which involves a streamlining of outside and inside. It creates a channel inside us between nature as received and welcomed through the senses, and these same senses as an outlet for emotion and feeling in the artwork which is then produced out of that initial stimulation. It is as if the gates which had never been opened are identified and we give ourselves permission to turn the key. The dual pressure from nature and the group creating together induces an atmosphere which allows the process to happen. The participants find that their senses are open and their creativity is released. Such experiences are life-changing; they achieve an inner transformation which is irreversible and indelible. Teachers who have had this experience are capable of communicating it to their pupils in ways that totally transform their presence in the classroom.

However, the number of children and teachers who have been touched in this way is minimal because the movement is so tiny, so unrecognised and so under-resourced. What needs to happen is a new partnership between the private,

---

[96] One teacher wrote: 'The experience encouraged me to write and to re-open the creative instincts in me, which had largely been subdued by the pressing demands of school and family life. I felt moved back in time in my spirit to a period when I was more open to the promptings of my own nature than the demands of the outside world.' Quoted in Cannon, *Promoting 'Lifetime Writers' in Primary Classrooms*, 2006, p. 55.

business and education sectors. Pushkin has worked twice with the business sector and the model has transferred well in these contexts as within the education cycle. It is only when our schools convince those who are meeting them as employers and partners that they have been given a rounded education, that these forces will begin to invest in such education. This, in turn, will persuade governments and departments of education to recognise that this methodology needs to become an essential part of every teacher-training programme. Immediate steps should be taken to make it possible for all trainee teachers to benefit from such an experience. The Pushkin movement is only the beginning of a revolution – not only in education, but in parenting, healthcare, business and politics, right into the very structures of our democracy.

Their conviction is quite simple: creative activity and the release of imagination can set us free. The Pushkin Trust has developed an almost foolproof methodology: bring people together in a beautiful place, give them the time and the stimulus to enjoy this experience and express themselves freely, guide them through the natural environment in ways that reveal the miracle unfolding around them, and introduce them to the possibilities of artistic expression which can help them to give voice to what they have just experienced. The principal target has been the field of education and the vehicle for delivery is the creative arts and the natural environment, through professional facilitation.

Of course there is a continuing argument about the real meaning of creativity. Theorists differ about emphasis on self-expression and work-of-art. Is it enough to pour out my feeling on a page or are there standards against which every artistic endeavour must be measured? The Pushkin method is not guaranteed to produce great artists, nor is it geared towards the development of creativity in society which will allow our children to compete with other countries in big business and entrepreneurial originality. Such definitions of creativity, which are fashionable in educational circles at present because they are seen as untapped resources to be detected and promoted, are valuable certainly but they are not the most important results of imagination:

> The functional interest in creativity, as a means of generating creative capital and ultimately supporting the economic life of a country, has fuelled international trends in curricula and planning in recent times ... However this international pendulum-swing in favour of this type of creativity is confining. In this functional light creativity is about generating a product. In a sense it is 'applied creativity.' The Pushkin Trust does not identify with this narrow focus but believes that true creativity should be free-floating and untrammelled, concerning itself with opening up possibilities and ideas and the development of the person, in the holistic sense. It believes that the creative process develops, enhances and extends the person, so that a person is made more 'whole' because of the creative experience. The pursuit of creativity is essential, it believes, for its own sake and not because of a resultant end product.[97]

Imagination and the creative impulse are released in a child not so that they can become a great artist but so that they can become themselves. For the Pushkin movement, creativity and imagination are the primary sources for the development of personality, and once the person has been touched by such originality they can then discover any and every possibility in their lives. Education is not primarily for national growth or productivity, it is for personal development and the release of unique potential. If every child in the country were to discover themselves at this level, then there would be no limit to the progress which could be made. This is why the Pushkin formula should be embraced

---

[97] Cannon, pp. 349–50.

by all education authorities and absorbed into the machinery of education in a thoroughly organic way so that it will be impossible for teachers of the future to escape from its liberating influence. 'The Pushkin rationale for pursuing creativity is that creative expression is essential if a person is to be fully alive.'[98]

The soul of any society can be found in its education system, which elaborates the values they wish to inculcate. Unless we put the child and the child's growth towards wholeness at the centre of our vision, our philosophies of education are askew. Perhaps now, because they have no money to finance the gargantuan and the immense, the powers that be will have to turn to a more modest model – one that is already tried and tested and would not cost too much to introduce. The breakdown of ancient and unsustainable structures can provide the setting for the emergence of new paradigms. Given that we have all this wisdom primed to be put in place, why do we persist in reproducing systems of education doomed to failure? Not only are they doomed to failure educationally, they are economically disastrous because they are built on unsustainable models. Perhaps the recession can work in favour of Pushkin. The methodology which has been developed by the Pushkin Trust could be the most economical way of introducing creativity into our schools.

How can this happen? It is very simple. The child (both in the classroom and as the 'child' in the adult) is key to the regeneration of our society for this twenty-first century in Ireland. A programme, with the working title of 'Inspired Education', should be designed, using the Pushkin model, to augment the existing professional development of a teacher, by complementing their teacher training programmes (and later in-service courses) with experiential workshops. As the teacher (and, hopefully, the parent) finds ways to connect with their own creative source, so this energy will

---

[98] Ibid., p. 350.

flow into the world of 'inspired education' and will benefit greatly the well-being and growth towards wholeness of all our children.

Inspired teaching, from the outset, opens the realm of the imagination, so that the living of life becomes an 'art' in itself. This art releases our potential and gives us the confidence to relate not only to ourselves but to all life around us. We also become, through this release of creativity in ourselves, problem solvers, lateral thinkers and lively entrepreneurial spirits, as a beneficial by-product for the economy!

Pushkin has developed the kind of intervention in favour of holistic maturation of the child that would be less costly and more effective than anything ever before envisaged. It offers a template which uses imagination as its key and promotes creativity as the single greatest asset of our people. This does not mean that we downgrade or sideline any of the other necessary aspects of education, such as literacy, numeracy or science; it simply means the provision of another essential element which develops the whole personality of the child centred upon the creative spirit, which also enhances every aspect of what they do in school and in living every aspect of their lives.

In every county of Ireland there are beautiful estates, forests, gardens, interpretive centres, museums, seacoasts and natural resorts which are underutilised. A team from the Pushkin Trust could visit schools all over the country and identify such places, round up artists and environmentalists, give these and the teachers a hands-on experience of the Pushkin method, and introduce an epidemic of creativity into our schools. It wouldn't need huge investment because we already have all that is necessary at our disposal. It only needs a change of mindset in the departments of education for the whole island of Ireland to introduce, promote and support a template for creative education as a lynchpin in the curriculum for every school. Such transformation will not occur through government departments unless there is a demand for this to happen from the business sector and from the adult world, which must by now be aware of just how anachronistic, stultifying and ineffective the present system has become.

We are talking about developing the whole person of the child. Every person should be offered such an experience of the release of the creative principle in their personal lives, so that they, in turn, can introduce it into the workplace or wherever they happen to be. The Pushkin initiative acts as a catalyst which engages imagination, releases creativity and enables the full expression of the whole person. When we describe this process as a paradigm, we are eschewing all notions of a prescriptive formulae. The magic has to happen on each occasion as a unique event in the life of the particular person. What the facilitators provide is the ambiance, the setting, the structures and the incentive that will allow it to happen. What Pushkin supplies here is the oil to infiltrate and lubricate already existing structures and organisations. There is nothing preset about the paradigm. It is not the answer in itself; it is the way to get to the answer. In each area and at each different time it has to be custom-designed to fit the local profile, the times and circumstances which prevail and the particular persons who present themselves.

Every teacher in every primary school throughout the country should have the opportunity during their training, or whenever they choose during their subsequent career, to have a Pushkin experience either at Baronscourt or at some other centre in the country which is designated, equipped and funded by the Department of Education. These teachers should then be responsible for organising similar experiences for the children in their own schools. This can happen by their choosing some place near to the school where they can assemble environmentalists and artists, who have also been immersed in the spirit of Pushkin, and who can recreate for the children an encounter with nature and a release of creativity akin to what has been happening at

Baronscourt over the last twenty-five years. This would mean that in a very few years a release of imagination in our schools would supply our children with all they need to fashion and face our future. If this became the template for education on the whole island of Ireland, we would become the envy of the rest of the world in terms of our people, who would be the most imaginative, creative and integrated persons, simply for having been put firmly in touch with their own creative source.

It should be possible to build upon the work of the regional leaders in their existing areas at present (Belfast, Tyrone, Antrim, Donegal, Longford and Dublin), thereby developing 'hubs of inspiration' which could replicate the Baronscourt experience in ever-expanding satellites. Pathways connecting these hubs should then open up as teachers share their experiences digitally.[99] These support networks for teachers throughout Ireland would deepen and channel the flow of the 'creative spirit', and become embedded in the education system and its curriculum both North and South. We have to carve out effective spaces in the curriculum for the trickle of imagination. Every minute of every day is full up with learning: the core subjects of the curriculum, homework, cramming, examinations, points awarded for examinations – we've no time to be children, we've grown up before we were allowed to know what was happening. Many of our greatest writers have only been so because they were tried and found wanting, even sometimes rejected, by the official system. Ireland should be recognising that our greatest natural resource is imaginative capacity. We should be inventing ways of educating which would nourish and encourage this potential.

It does seem that the Pushkin movement has the right ingredients to fire the imagination, awaken the senses and

---

[99] Interesting literature on this can be found in the *Rethinking Education* series, Vol. II: Marie Martin, *Learning by Wandering, An Ancient Irish Perspective for a Digital World* (Bern: Peter Lang, 2010).

encourage self-expression. It inspires confidence and engenders enthusiasm, spontaneity, fun; it provokes curiosity, and instils motivation at the same time as providing task-oriented self-discipline. Nothing focuses the attention more than accomplishing a worthwhile creative task. There was huge affirmation from schools, both teachers and children, about the creative energy this movement unleashed in people's personal lives and in the groups involved – teachers at both ends of the spectrum were affected: those who have been in the classroom for years and who reconnected with their own creative voice, and student teachers from the teacher training colleges, who found themselves inspired by it. The time has come to spread that influence wider and further, without losing anything of the quality and depth of the personal experience.

This does not mean trying to establish an alternative or parallel system of education. It means injecting into the established educational system an essential element which will transform it. As such, it might be thought of as a nutrient that feeds energy into the system so that the children can flourish; or as an enzyme which when mixed like yeast into the dough has the effect of leavening the batch. Such a spirit needs to pervade the perhaps necessarily monolithic structure of any educational system. What is proposed is the amalgamation of the best in both. Without the magic of creativity, education is without spark or zest. Ireland is awash with creativity. Our educational system needs to harness and make provision for that energy. If it does not do so, the opposite happens: creativity is quenched. We can produce very clever, very efficient, very obedient automatons, but the essential spark of imagination is missing. If we succeed in flooding the already existing structures with imaginative life, every aspect and every part of how and what we learn could be enhanced.

CHAPTER NINE

Cherishing and Challenging

> If one would have a friend, one must also want to wage war for him: and in order to wage war, one must be able to be an enemy. One should honour even the enemy in one's friend. Can you step up close to your friend without going over to him? In one's friend one should have one's best enemy. You should be closest to him in your heart when you strive against him ... May your compassion be a divining: that you might first know whether your friend wants compassion. Perhaps he loves in you the unbroken eye and the glance of eternity. May compassion for the friend conceal itself under a hard shell; you shall lose a tooth biting on it. Thus it will have its subtlety and sweetness. Are you pure air and solitude and bread and medicine for your friend?[100]

Cherishing and challenging have always been the two poles between which education has had to make its tightrope walk. The history of our education system in Ireland is bestrewn with aberrations where too much cherishing on the one hand led to criminal affairs between adults and minors, and too much challenging on the other led to wholesale physical abuse and sadistic punishment. Being aware of the pitfalls and knowing how to hold the balance is essential to successful education. Every teacher is faced by such a Scylla and Charybdis experience. We risk being smashed against the hard, rocky cliff of challenge and being drowned in the whirlpool of infatuation. The skill to sail our ship between these two sources of educational destruction must be acquired.

---

[100] Friedrich Nietzsche, *Thus Spoke Zarathustra*, Graham Parkes, trans. (Oxford: Oxford University Press, 2005), pp. 49–50.

The corresponding truth is that if a teacher does not have such a problem then they are unlikely ever to be inspirational. In some very precise and magical way, your students have to be enthralled by you if the educational relationship is to happen. This is not a bad thing; in fact, it is inevitable. Education happens through such human transmission. We must not be afraid of the challenge. Just because so many wreckages have taken place either against the cliff or within the whirlpool does not mean that we should lower the voltage on the educational journey. Having anodyne teachers who inspire no emotional reaction whatsoever from their pupils does not place the educational experiment into safe hands; on the contrary, it extinguishes it completely. Boring purveyors of knowledge in a classroom are no antidote to the dangers of educational overkill. There must be in any genuine educational relationship an electricity which jumpstarts the emerging life of the pupil. With all the legitimate and understandable present-day concerns about child protection, we must be careful not to eliminate the essential educational magic without which the learner can remain forever inert and unawakened.

True education is our only way forward and what we must do is ensure that all our teachers are trained and competent to exercise the very delicate relationship which is their unique and demanding task. Basically speaking, this means training them to walk the exhilarating and dangerous path between the cliff of challenge and the abyss of cherishing. Which means training teachers, body and soul, heart and mind, in establishing genuine educational relationship. Often children can quite unwarrantedly project an almost mythological status onto the adults in whose charge they find themselves. Without a full understanding of this projection, teachers can misappropriate and use it to selfish ends.

When I was studying for the Higher Diploma in Education in 1974, one of the important names in the

Philosophy of Education was Carl Rogers, whose book, *Freedom to Learn: A View of What Education Might Become*, was required reading on any course about teaching or the psychology of education.[101] He refers so specifically to Martin Buber in his writings that, in America, the two writers were closely identified. And as far as human relationships are concerned, Rogers' notion of 'empathy', which he applies to both the areas of education and psychotherapy, became synonymous with Buber's notion of 'I-Thou'.

From a reading of *Freedom to Learn*, it becomes clear that Rogers intends to transfer the relationship of empathy, which he finds so successful in psychotherapy, to the educational encounter between students and teachers. In this book, Rogers gives both the theory of 'educational empathy' and various examples of its success in action. The argument centres around the proposition that if this works so well in psychotherapy, then it should be equally valid in education:

> If in therapy, the client perceives his therapist as real and genuine, as one who likes, prizes and empathically understands him, self-learning and therapeutic change are facilitated.[102]

Therapy is thus identified with the learning situation, and the relationship which makes for most effective therapy is transposed to the classroom. The connection between both situations and Buber's philosophy is stated explicitly in the introduction to part II of this work:

> Chapter 4 could be summed up in a beautiful statement by Martin Buber, who says the good teacher '... must be a really existing man and he must be really

---

[101] Carl Rogers, *Freedom to Learn* (Columbus, Ohio: Charles E. Merrill Publishing Company, 1969).
[102] Ibid., p. 116.

present to his pupils; he educates through contact. Contact is the primary word of education.'

The chain of reduction from Buber's 'I-Thou' relationship is now logical and complete. The 'empathy' that is the translation of 'I-Thou' in a psychotherapeutic situation also establishes the specific relationship that should exist between the teacher and the 'learner':

This attitude of standing in the other's shoes, of viewing the world through the student's eyes, is almost unheard of in the classroom. One could listen to thousands of ordinary classroom interactions without coming across one instance of clearly communicated, sensitively accurate, empathic understanding ... The example I have cited also indicates how deeply appreciative students feel when they are simply *understood* – not evaluated, not judged, simply understood from their own point of view, not the teacher's.[103]

For Rogers, the pedagogical relationship is a horizontal and unanchored link of acceptance and 'empathy' between the teacher and the student. The teacher is not required to judge, evaluate or confirm the student, he or she is merely required to understand with sensitivity. Rogers would seem to expect his teacher to show no reaction other than sensitive and sympathetic understanding, with no reference to the objective or concrete justice of any particular situation. This is suffocation through cherishing and not educational relationship. This is one of the main reasons for rejecting 'empathy' as an adequate description of the 'I-Thou' in education. In the face of such errors of theory and practice it is understandable that Buber should be blamed for initiating a situation of chaos. In an article called 'Education

---

[103] Ibid., p. 112.

is not I-Thou', Eugene Borowitz states clearly this point of view:

> With all these reinforcements of contemporary infantilism, none is called upon more frequently or sanctimoniously than Martin Buber's teaching of the holiness of the I-Thou encounter. That most people who cite Buber have not read him, and even more misunderstand him, has little to do with his social effect. That Buber is 'in' makes it all the more important to review his ideas.[104]

Borowitz goes so far as to claim that a correct reading of Buber would show that, whereas the latter promoted the 'I-Thou' relationship in every other area of life, the one exception was the area of education:

> Martin Buber, however, was not an orthodox Buberian. With regard to education, he made a major break with his own system. Education, Buber taught, for all that it must centre about the person, education is not I-Thou ... He insists that in the educator's movement toward the student, he may not try to set up a fully reciprocal relationship with him. The moment the educator is as much thou to his charges as they are to him, education is over and friendship beings.[105]

It must be obvious from the very existence of such contradictory viewpoint that some clarification of Buber's position is both necessary and urgent. We are fortunate to have a dialogue between Rogers and Buber, moderated and published by Maurice Friedman, in which they discuss the

---

[104] Eugene Borowitz, 'Education is not "I-Thou"', *Religious Education* (1971), pp. 326–31.
[105] Ibid., p. 328–9.

very issue concerning us. The dialogue took place in the University of Michigan in 1957 at a Midwest Conference on Martin Buber. Friedman says that he was so struck by the apparent resemblances between the thought of Rogers and Buber that he devoted three pages of the 'Psychotherapy' chapter in his biography of Buber to a comparison of their attitudes towards psychology. This dialogue, however, reveals the fundamental differences which underlie a superficial similarity. Buber asserts that an anchorless relationship of empathy, in which no exigency is imposed other than that of understanding the present situation of the 'other', is never enough to fulfil real relationship, or genuine dialogue, at any level. There is the 'potentiality' of the person which must be catered for, even if this means refusing to confirm the present state of the other person. There is also the fact of existence, the common ground, the soil, an objective reality, which cannot be gainsaid in favour of some private world, made up of and understood by the two people who are interrelating.

Although Buber admits that his lack of experience in the field of psychotherapy does not allow him to pronounce judgement on Rogers' use of empathy in this sphere, he does insist that the transposition of this relationship to the field of education represents a complete misinterpretation of his own thought. Buber would never accept that a relationship of empathy and acceptance was all that is required of a teacher. He would repudiate the presentation in *Freedom to Learn* of what is supposed to be summed up in his statement that 'contact is the primary word of education'. The relationship of empathy, proposed by Rogers, was shown to be inadequate to the educational encounter because it was an unwarranted application of a relationship which he found successful in one restricted area, to another situation which bears little resemblance to this field.

In a short story called 'Tomorrow and Tomorrow and Tomorrow and So Forth', John Updike describes a teacher, Mark Prosser, who finds a girl passing a note to a friend during his English class. He takes the note and reads it. The note says that the girl 'loves' him. He tells her to see him after class. He is secretly fond of the girl and is deeply touched by her note. After class he lectures her about not writing down her secret thoughts and about being careful not to abuse the word 'love'. She cries. He returns to the teacher's common room in very good form. Here he is told that the girl, Gloria Angstrom, has been caught passing such notes during all her classes that morning, in an effort to gauge the effect they would have on all her different teachers.

Such an anecdote describes the kind of ambiguity which should always be considered in the mentality of the oppressed. The kind of empathy which Rogers proposes in his theory of educational relationship does not cater for such ambiguity. The teacher must always act directly, must always trust his students and believe in their potential, but it must be an open-eyed trust which takes a comprehensive view of the total situation, especially the ambiguous nature of the student's position as an oppressed and underdeveloped being.

Education can never be 'empathy' in this sense. And the reason is that empathy overemphasises cherishing at the expense of challenging. Most would agree that any relationship begins with acceptance. There can be no dialogue at all, and no education, if trust is not established in the first place. However, this 'acceptance' or 'trust' is only the beginning. The second element is the equally important notion of 'confirmation'.[106] Every one of us needs to be confirmed both as what we are, and as what we can become, by another person. Confirmation establishes us as persons in our own right, and without it humanity can scarcely unfold. An anchorless relationship of empathy, in which no exigency is imposed other than that of understanding the present situation of the student, is never enough.

---

[106] Martin Buber, *The Knowledge of Man* (London: Allen & Unwin, 1965), p. 68.

Confirmation 'of what we can become' may, indeed, involve the rejection of what we actually are, so that the future reality has room to emerge: 'A conflict with a pupil is the supreme test for the educator.'[107] Conflicts have an educational value as long as they occur in a healthy atmosphere of mutual confidence. The teacher must use insight during these battles for truth. If the teacher wins the battle they have to help the pupil to endure defeat. And if we cannot overcome the pupil's will, then we must find the word of love that will make the conflict part of the educational process.

In an essay on friendship, R. W. Emerson expresses a similar thought: 'I hate,' he says, 'where I looked for a manly furtherance, or at least a manly resistance, to find a mush of concession. Better be a nettle in the side of your friend than his echo.' Confirmation implies the rejection of 'seeming' in favour of 'being'. The 'potential' of the person must be catered for, even if this means refusing to confirm the present state of this person. There is also the fact of existence, the common ground, the soil, the objective reality, which cannot be refuted in favour of some private world, made up of, and understood by, one person or two people. The responsibility for the total situation lies with the teacher. The pupil is responsible only for his or her own presence. He or she has no responsibility for the relationship itself. The teacher is required to monitor the relationship from both sides.

Genuine contact with the teacher makes the child send out feelers or tendrils like a young plant, which the teacher must not allow to take root. Such anchorage is what the child longs for, and the teacher's responsibility is to prevent this child from grafting onto any being other than their own. The teacher must not allow the dependence of the child to act as confirmation for present being; this dependence must be transformed into a bridge over which the child can walk

---

[107] Aubrey Hodes, *Encounter with Martin Buber* (London: Penguin, 1975), p. 138.

towards a future of their own. This can be done by disentangling the feelers that encircle us as we teach, transforming these from tentacles that drag the object downwards, to grappling irons that draw the owner upwards.

These feelers, which reach out towards mature being, come from that instinct of communion which is expressive of the core of the child's being. They are ropes which stretch from the centre towards another centre. The role of the teacher is to help the child to walk this tightrope stretched between them, not in the direction of the teacher, but back into the centre from where it comes, and which is now accessible because this contact has opened the way. When the pupil has embodied and appropriated the centre point delineated by the instinct for communion reaching out towards the teacher, this appropriation of their ownmost form will automatically release them from the spell of thraldom, which is no more than the desire to find a more solid centre elsewhere. Such release will signal the successful completion of the educational process.

Until this plenitude of personal being has been reached, it is the responsibility of the teacher to see that every gesture of communication made by the child becomes a source of growth and development towards that goal. We re-direct the thraldom for the child's own enrichment back to its own source within themselves.

CHAPTER TEN

Father de Pradts and Miss Jean Brodie

I was frightened. Just to think of the pulls and tugs, like riptides, that must be going on inside of him was scary. Dense as I might have been about him before, I knew for certain ... that what he wanted deep down was to take me up to the mountains or down to the seashore. But he could never admit it to me – no matter what he thought I'd done – and he probably could never admit it to himself. I also knew that I could never really speak to him again. How can you talk to someone when you know what their real meaning is and they won't ever acknowledge it to you – and you can't.[108]

The two people included in the title of this chapter had a very powerful influence over the pupils in their charge. And yet, their exercise of this power had the 'inevitable consequence of disintegration'. 'When an unbridled schoolmistress with advanced ideas is in her prime the classroom can take on a new identity and no one can predict what will happen': this sentence appears on the cover of a 1965 edition of Muriel Spark's novel, *The Prime of Miss Jean Brodie*.[109] Miss Brodie's battle cry is: 'Give me a girl at an impressionable age and she is mine for life.' All her pupils are the *crème de la crème*. She devotes her life to this process of 'putting old heads on your young shoulders':

> Miss Brodie had already selected her favourites, or
> rather those whom she could trust; or rather those

---

[108] James Kirkwood, *Good Times/Bad Times* (New York: Fawcett Crest Books, 1969), p. 266.
[109] Muriel Spark, *The Prime of Miss Jean Brodie* (London: Penguin, 1965).

whose parents she could trust not to lodge complaints about the more advanced and seditious aspects of her educational policy, these parents being either too enlightened to complain or too unenlightened, or too awed by their good fortune ... Miss Brodie's special girls were taken home to tea and bidden not to tell the others, they were taken into her confidence, they understood her private life and her feud with the headmistress. They learned what troubles in her career Miss Brodie had encountered on their behalf. 'It is for the sake of you girls – my influence, now, in the years of my prime.'[110]

Jean Brodie enjoys 'her girls' at an age when they were unable to resist her charms. Instead of concentrating her attention and energy on the business of their development, she hypnotised them into a situation where their lives, their interest, their energies, were exhausted by her. The weight of this relationship was too heavy, too exhilarating, too immediately satisfying to allow for any development of themselves: 'The girls, chosen out by Miss Brodie, for her special attention, found, later on in life, that their days with her were the happiest of their lives. Miss Brodie saw to it that this should be the case.'

Nor was she simply contented with this stunting of their present growth, which allowed them to act as mirrors to her own. She also insisted on extending her influence to the formation and direction of their futures. Each one was expected to fulfil one of the secret ambitions harboured by Miss Brodie in her own life, but surrendered by her in that gesture of sacrifice with which she gave herself up to the formation of youth. When a local artist falls in love with her and asks her to pose for him, she sends one of her girls instead. The artist paints Miss Brodie in the girl. Even the girl sees this in the portrait.

---

[110] Ibid., p. 26.

But soon both of them accept the fateful substitution and the girl becomes his lover.

This 'will to power' and this 'Eros' are very definite possibilities in the life of any educator. They may be less obvious and exaggerated in other cases, but if they are present they destroy the educational relationship. The truth is that those who are victims of such inclinations have no real interest in the people they confront. The children do not exist for them as unique and particular entities. They exist only as the teacher imagines they should be.

> I know of leaders who with their grip, not only cast into confusion the plasma of the growing human being but also disintegrate it radically, so that it can no longer be moulded. They relish this power of their influence, and at the same time deceive themselves and their herd into imagining they are moulders of youthful souls, and call on Eros, who is inaccessible to the *profanum vulgus*, as the tutelary god of this work.[111]

Miss Brodie was forced to retire on the grounds that she had been teaching fascism: 'Of course,' said Miss Brodie, 'this political question was only an excuse ... It was my educational policy they were up against which had reached its perfection in my prime. I was dedicated to my girls, as you know.' What is frightening is the sincerity.

Other forms of the 'lame-winged Eros', to be distinguished from the genuine dialogue of education, have also been described by Buber:

> Many years I have wandered through the land of men, and have not yet reached the end of studying the varieties of the 'erotic man' (as the vassal of the broken-winged one at times describes himself). There

---

[111] Buber, *Between Man and Man*, p. 49.

a lover stamps around and is in love only with his own passion. There one is wearing his differentiated feelings like medal-ribbons. There one is enjoying the adventures of his own fascinating effect. There one is gazing enraptured at the spectacle of his own supposed surrender. There one is collecting excitement. There one is displaying his power. There one is preening himself with borrowed vitality. There one is delighting to exist simultaneously as himself and as an idol very unlike himself. There one is warming himself at the blaze of what has fallen to his lot. There one is experimenting. And so on and on – the manifold monologists and their mirrors, in the apartment of the most intimate dialogue![112]

Can any teacher read this paragraph without at some time during it holding his breath? Surely every one of us is guilty of at least one such urge at times? Buber does not claim that these are either unusual or irredeemable in the teacher. He does hold that we must become aware of them if we are to prepare ourselves for the real task of education. Where one or other of these motives supplies the basic energy to our work, the educational relationship is destroyed.

Henry de Montherlant, in his novel *The Boys*, describes a subtle version of such destruction in the person of Father de Pradts.[113] He is a Catholic priest who does not believe in God but whose one passion in life is to devote himself exclusively to boys and to live among them. In the society in which he lived 'it was the cassock which best guaranteed that life'. And so, he spent his whole life as a priest, without believing in God, which no one seemed to notice, first as

[112] Ibid.
[113] Henry de Montherlant, *The Boys* (London: Weidenfeld and Nicholson, 1974), English translation of *Les Garçons* (Paris: Editions Gallimard, 1969).

second in command of a fashionable boys school in Paris and later on looking after less well-to-do children in the Morbihan.

When a priest lacks ambition, the author tells us, it is either from spiritual detachment or it is because his passion lies elsewhere. This was the case with Father de Pradts. He knew it from his earliest years and he devoted his life to achieving his special kind of happiness: 'It was from the "young" that he drew his strength and inspiration – he had never for a moment weighed his career against his taste for educational life, which condemned him to obscurity.' So 'Father de Pradts lived on the one hand gorged with small boys and on the other hand much respected.' His conduct with the boys was always honourable. In fact, he was very gifted in his handling of them. He demanded nothing of them except his constant presence among them and the pleasure he derived from regulating their brittle and unformed lives. 'Specialist in the drama of the soul, not only in healing them, but provoking them, he was the dilettante of emotional storms and rivalries.' He devoted his whole attention to his 'youngsters', entertaining them, being loved by them, and being useful to them.

> The presence of Father de Pradts had been on the whole beneficial. Beneficial because of his constant efforts to lift the boys, not towards a Christian life, but towards a life of independence and integrity ... Beneficial because of the genuine affection he felt even for those who did not have attractive faces. His was a rare gift: instinctively, that is to say with instantaneous acumen, whatever the circumstances, he put himself in their place. This being so, almost anything they did seemed to him natural and normal considering their age ... And over and above all this, he had the keenest sense of equity, so dear to children. With this understanding, this friendliness, and this sense of

justice, it can be said without hesitation that Father
de Pradts was beneficent.[114]

He never did anything to harm the Church because he was
grateful to it for supplying him with the precise situation
which made him perfectly happy. He never made any
demands on the boys. His modest ambition, as far as they
were concerned, was to be remembered as a 'father'; an
ambition which, the author tells us, seems 'unbelievable in
its mediocrity, almost laughable, but which was not, because
it was the fruit of a genuine passion'.[115]

And so, it might be said, what is there to complain about?
Here are two needs which seem to complement each other
perfectly. The boys need to be educated and Father de Pradts
needs to educate them – what more could we want? But the
truth is that the educational relationship can never be the
fruit of merely natural inclination. The author quotes Valéry
in the beginning of his book as saying that 'any view of
things which fails to recognise their oddity is false', and one
of the aims of this novel is to elucidate the essential oddity
of Father de Pradts' passion to educate.

> One does not remain unaffected by a long period
> spent exclusively with people very different from
> oneself in age and social background: the influence of
> the less developed rubs off on the more developed.
> During his nine years of provincial, not to say a trifle
> rustic, dealings with boys, Father de Pradts's mind
> had contracted somewhat, and in many respects
> grown dimmer. It was a cultivated mind, but it was
> totally lacking in curiosity, and it lived on its cultural
> capital.[116]

---

[114] Ibid., p. 71.
[115] Ibid., p. 270.
[116] Ibid., p. 269.

His education was the attempt to establish a paradise in which the boys would be enough for him and enough for each other. The relationship was certainly one of real empathy, but a stagnant empathy, which he kept from palling by his genius for entertainment and for provoking the kind of emotional atmosphere which made it so artificially exciting.

Instead of the genuine dialogue of education, which establishes a real contact with the being of youth *as youth*, and points the way towards real unity of being and personhood, this was a relationship of mutual convenience, which, if anything, reduced the teacher to the level of childhood. Since neither term of the relationship was real, the dialogue between them was also unreal:

> These children who said nothing about their conduct, and this priest who said nothing about his faith, made up an assembly of veiled figures interweaving, a kind of masked ball of black robes and bare legs.[117]

Father de Pradts loved his charges and he understood them so well that he excused everything they did. He never questioned them about their behaviour, their growth, their life of the spirit. He, in his turn, never talked about his faith, never communicated any higher purpose. The boys sufficed. His was an attempt to confirm them in their being as youth, instead of being the establishment of a trust which would goad them towards genuine becoming.

The attempt of Miss Jean Brodie to put old heads on young shoulders, and of Father de Pradts to keep young heads on young shoulders for as long as possible, are both deviations from the educational norm. But what exactly is that norm? Are we to conclude that no one can teach unless the underlying motivation is superhumanly pure?

---

[117] Ibid., p. 67.

Buber would claim that even in the case of the greatest educators, there is bound to be a certain mixture of motivation. He points out that the 'unity of being' which founds the genuine will to educate involves a certain asceticism which refuses to allow the 'lame-winged Eros' to interfere with the work of education proper. What all teachers have to acquire is 'the special humility of the educator for whom the life and particular being of all his pupils is the decisive factor'.

As teachers we are required to examine our motivation and become aware of the variety of possible needs within ourselves which could interfere with our educational task. There is no violent opposition between education and Eros. Both are movements towards the other person. The asceticism here involved is not the annihilation of these realities but the harmonisation of all faculties within the personality. Spiritual unity is achieved, not by the domination of any one faculty or power over the rest, but by the harmonisation of all faculties within the personality.

> The objectively ascetic character of the sphere of education must not, however, be misunderstood as being so separated from the instinct to power and from Eros that no bridge can be flung from them to it. I have already pointed out how very significant Eros can be to the educator without corroding his work. What matters here is the threshold and the transformation which takes place on it. It is not the church alone which has a testing threshold on which a man is transformed or becomes a lie. But in order to be able to carry out this every renewed transition from sphere to sphere he must have carried it out once in a decisive fashion and taken up in himself the essence of education.[118]

---

[118] Buber, *Between Man and Man*, pp. 122–3.

If educators really understand the precise realm of being for which they are responsible, they will be so struck by this reality that anything less than genuine educational relationship will be a cheap and unsatisfying substitute. Sacrifice and self-restraint are not enough. The teacher must be totally imbued with the genuine desire to educate. If not, this presence takes on an ambiguous shape, which is sensed by the student and makes direct and fruitful contact impossible. The teacher can also take advantage of the situation of thraldom and emotional dependence by using it as a force with which to mould the child in a certain way, instead of allowing the child to appropriate his or her 'ownmost form'. This need not be done in any obviously violent way. It is sufficient to simply withdraw support at a given moment and allow the child to be crushed beneath the weight of their own guilt and fragility. The first signs of emerging originality and personality can be withered back to the root simply by not providing them with the encouragement they need to offset the innate depreciation and reprobation which surround them in the faltering psychology of the oppressed: 'Self-depreciation is another characteristic of the oppressed which derives from their internalisation of the opinion the oppressors hold of them.'[119] The child automatically expects disapproval from the educator for any manifestation of originality or any form of self-affirmation. Unless the educator shows positive approval, the child will assume disapproval. The mere withholding of approval can, therefore, ensure that the child crushes whatever fails to evoke a positive response. In this way, the educator can subtly direct growth in whatever direction he or she chooses.

In other words, Buber suggests that both Father de Pradts and Miss Jean Brodie could have been transformed into genuine educators. Although we have condemned their actual educational practice, this does not mean that we

---

[119] Freire, *Pedagogy of the Oppressed*, 1972, p. 38

have excluded them from the educational sphere. A transformation is required, but one which is certainly possible.

Unfortunately, it has happened all too frequently that teachers are unaware of their own cratetic, or cynical, motivation. We persuade ourselves that our desire to educate is genuine and refuse to admit, even to ourselves, that the hidden well-spring of our teaching life is a passion of the soul, which would have to be elaborated in another dimension if it were to be prevented from corroding our best efforts. Such hidden motivation compromises the educational situation. The teacher has become yet one more oppressor instead of being the one who can release the person from their condition of being oppressed. It is all the more harmful because coming in the guise of a liberator, you reinforce the chains of oppression. From the point of view of the educator, the danger of falsification arises because the educator has ceased to treat the student's desire to be dominated or enjoyed as 'a wrong condition needing to be cured'.[120]

The fact that we may never act upon these hidden motives in no way legitimises our educational endeavours. The hidden passion which motivates it will always colour our activity, even if we ourselves are quite blind to its presence. 'These people abstain,' as Nietzsche puts it, 'but the bitch sensuality glares enviously out of all they do. This restless beast follows them even into the heights of their virtue and the depths of their cold spirit. And how nicely the bitch sensuality knows how to beg for a piece of spirit when a piece of flesh is denied her.'[121]

Even when this corroding force is not apparent to the teacher, it is often sensed intuitively by the pupil. Thraldom is the raw material from which educational contact is generated. Unless the teacher, who is entirely responsible

---

[120] Buber, *Between Man and Man*, p. 123.
[121] Nietzsche, 'Of Chastity', *Thus Spoke Zarathustra*, p. 81.

for this realm of being, understands this situation from both sides and uses it in a way which leads the pupil to full appropriation of his or her own form of selfhood, it can become counter-productive. To ignore or suppress this reality in the educational relationship is to neglect the fundamental structure of the pedagogical encounter and to dissipate one of the major forces in the development of youth.

CHAPTER ELEVEN

The Special Humility of the Educator

And then there was St Kevin and the blackbird.
The saint is kneeling, arms stretched out, inside
His cell, but the cell is narrow, so

One turned-up palm is out the window, stiff
As a crossbeam, when a blackbird lands
And lays in it and settles down to nest.

Kevin feels the warm eggs, the small breast, the tucked
Neat head and claws and, finding himself linked
Into the network of eternal life,

Is moved to pity: now he must hold his hand
Like a branch out in the sun and rain for weeks
Until the young are hatched and fledged and flown.

*

And since the whole thing's imagined anyhow,
Imagine being Kevin. Which is he?
Self-forgetful or in agony all the time

From the neck on out down through his hurting forearms?
Are his fingers sleeping? Does he still feel his knees?
Or has the shut-eyed blank of underearth

Crept up through him? Is there distance in his head?
Alone and mirrored clear in love's deep river,
'To labour and not to seek reward,' he prays,

A prayer his body makes entirely
For he has forgotten self, forgotten bird
And on the riverbank forgotten the river's name.[122]

Seamus Heaney, 'St Kevin and The Blackbird'

E ducation is essentially a personal communication. It cannot be achieved in any other way. As a human relationship, our contact with our pupils can be as combustible as any other. To harness these connections in a way that is helpful for the child and conducive to the genuine educational relationship on which all pedagogy depends, we have to understand fully the situation in which we find ourselves.

As teachers, we are responsible for both sides of this relationship; we have to monitor the educational encounter both for ourselves and for the child. The way we can achieve this is through what Buber calls the special humility of the educator. This humility comes not from a denial of the feelings we may have, nor from a suppression of them, but through a transformation towards 'a lofty asceticism' whereby they become stimuli towards another goal. This is the effect of 'the special humility of the educator'. Humility comes from the Latin word *humus* meaning 'ground'. Having one's feet firmly on the ground means understanding the precise realm for which one is responsible. In each one of these children placed before us we must see a potential person. Our job is to become midwives to that life which each child has a right to experience to the full.

Those who would say that this is an élitish notion which our society cannot afford are simply saying that our society cannot afford the luxury of genuine education. Anything less than direct communication between teacher and pupil is not education. Others will suggest that the number of teachers who are capable of such communication are small. Are we to restrict their influence to the tiny minority that they can

[122] Seamus Heaney, 'St Kevin and the Blackbird', *The Spirit Level* (London: Faber & Faber, 1996).

come into contact with directly? The answer is quite simple: no one can educate more people than they can come into contact with directly. Once asked whether this meant that all those who are not this person's students must remain excluded from their teaching, Buber replied:

> Not at all, for those who are transformed through his teaching are forthwith, one and all, apostles – even though they do not repeat anything of it, nor even proclaim the name of the teacher; as transformed men, they are apostles through their existence, and whatever they do is done in apostleship, through the essence of his teaching which they express therein. In the life of his friends, in the life of all who meet him, and thus to distant generation, immediacy is transmitted.[123]

The role of the teacher is to transmit immediacy. To do this a teacher must make direct and immediate contact with the student without turning that contact into an ego trip. This requires the kind of asceticism expressed in Seamus Heaney's poem about St Kevin, where the saint has to 'hold out his hand/... Until the young are hatched and fledged and flown.' Such a stance, such patience, such endurance, is the work of humility, that 'shut-eyed blank of underearth' which allows some reality other than our own to impose itself. The centre of power and movement is transferred to the space between ourselves and the other. This 'common ground' becomes the locus of truth. 'Experiencing the other side' means that our knowledge of the other becomes the regulating factor. The emphasis has shifted from preoccupation with monologue to engagement in dialogue. 'A transfusion has taken place after which a mere elaboration of subjectivity is never again possible or tolerable.'[124] If we, as educators, really

---

[123] Buber, *Pointing the Way*, p. 7.
[124] Ibid., p. 124.

understand the precise realm of being for which we are responsible, we will be so struck, so moved, by this reality that anything less than the genuine relationship of education will be a cheap and unsatisfying substitute. This new 'ground' of being will provide the base and the source of an effortless humility.

Nor does Buber claim that it is possible to start out on this mission without at some time soiling our hands. There is no violent opposition between education and Eros. Both are movements towards the other person. The asceticism here involved is not the annihilation of these realities. Spiritual unity is achieved, not by the domination of any one faculty or power over the rest, but by the harmonisation of all faculties within the personality.

> The objectively ascetic character of the sphere of education must not, however, be misunderstood as being so separated from the instinct to power and from Eros that no bridge can be flung from them to it. I have already pointed out how very significant Eros can be to the educator without corroding his work. What matters here is the threshold and the transformation which takes place on it. But in order to be able to carry out this ever renewed transition from sphere to sphere he must have carried it out once in a decisive fashion and taken up in himself the essence of education.[125]

Mistakes will be made, and perfection is not an essential preliminary:

> The basic position of Buber affirms that 'true purity is not the same as being untouched'. In other words, the moral man should not seek to maintain himself aloof from the troubling fight of life. He should dare

---

[125] Buber, *Between Man and Man*, p. 123.

to engage in it, dedicate himself to it, to the certain danger of dirtying his hands.[126]

However, it is one thing to soil one's hands in the course of an operation, it is quite another to arrive in the operating theatre with dirty hands. There is a distinction to be made between the possibility of man's fall in the pursuit of truth and the substitution of the pursuit of self for that truth. Though the good man does not exist, the good does. And the good of education demands that those engaging themselves in this particular struggle should arm themselves with some awareness of the form of this particular good.

A quotation from the section on 'humility' in one of Buber's books on Hasidism will provide an interesting marginal note:

> The humble man lives in each being and knows each being's manner and virtue ... Only living with the other is justice. Living with the other as a form of knowing is justice. Living with the other as a form of being is love ... But in truth love is all-comprehensive and sustaining and is extended to all the living without selection and distinction ... 'Every man has a light over him, and when the souls of two men meet, the two lights join each other and from them there goes forth one light. And this is called generation'.
>
> To feel the universal generation as a sea and oneself as a wave, that is the mystery of humility. ... The true humility which is meant here is no willed and practised virtue. It is nothing but an inner being, feeling, and expressing. Nowhere in it is there a compulsion, nowhere a self-humbling, a self-restraining, a self-resolve.[127]

---

[126] Ernst Simon in *The Philosophy of Martin Buber*, Paul Arthur Schillp and Maurice Friedman, eds. (Opencourt, Illinois: The Library of Living Philosophers, 1967), p. 572.

[127] Buber, *Hasidism and Modern Man*, Maurice Friedman, ed., trans. (New York: Harper Torchbooks, 1996), pp. 110–22.

The special humility of the educator is achieved by a kind of knowledge which allows us to understand our own unique being and the unique reality of every child, and allows us to be present to both in a way that submerges the petty gestures of our 'lame-winged Eros'. The asceticism here involved is not just an act of self-control based upon a consciousness of our inclinations. It must be more radical than that:

> There is an elemental experience which shatters at least the assurance of the erotic as well as the cratetic man, but sometimes does more, forcing its way at white-heat into the heart of the instinct and remoulding it. A reversal of the single instinct takes place, which does not eliminate it but reverses its system of direction.[128]

This 'reversal of the system of direction' is what turns the pride of Eros and the will to power into the 'special humility of the educator'.

> Such a reversal can be effected by the elemental experience with which the real process of education begins and on which it is based. I call it experiencing the other side.

As teachers, we have to know ourselves and know what we are trying to do. Armed with this double knowledge we can fulfil our task. There is a paradox which must be resolved before we begin to educate: education is the fully spontaneous presence of the teacher, and, at the same time, it requires careful critical analysis. We must submit both to the proportions and to the limits of education's 'special objectivity'. Unless we are prepared to unravel the subtle knot of such 'paradoxical legitimacy' with a great deal of

---

[128] Buber, *Between Man and Man*, p. 123.

patience, we cannot hope to understand the fragile reality with which we are engaged. Only those who are wholly alive and prepared to communicate this aliveness in its spontaneity to others with their whole being can really affect the life of a pupil. But we must be merciless with ourselves about naïve enthusiasm and good will. We must learn to be both spontaneous and reflective at the same time. Achieved spontaneity is the discipline we learn. Only those who know how to distinguish between reality and appearance, the genuine and the fake, in themselves and in their students, will be qualified to teach.

The teacher has to develop an instinctive flair for the style of the real presence of the other. This can never become a formula or a repeatable exercise. The 'other' remains always an unaccountable mystery that can never be known beforehand. The task of the teacher is to find the way towards embodiment and appropriation of ownmost form, the unique being of every person, which is always different in itself and different in its way of unfurling. What the child needs to know and to do in order to accomplish this task is generated and unveiled by direct contact with mature being, in this case that of the teacher, which has already gained such self-appropriation. The teacher is the one who is responsible for such contact. The educator uses 'realistic imagination' to detect the symptoms of this real being, the gestures which are expressive of this unique style of being. When, and as, the child appropriates his or her ownmost form, the teacher tests this mettle and confirms this manifestation of real presence.

In all this description of the teacher-student relationship, Buber uses the example of the true Zaddik or spiritual leader.

Each man has an infinite sphere of responsibility, responsibility before the infinite. He moves, he talks, he looks, and each of his movements, each of his words, each of his glances causes waves to surge in the happenings of the world: he cannot know how strong or how far-reaching. Each man with all his being and doing determines the fate of the world in a measure unknowable to him and all others; for the causality which we can perceive is indeed only a tiny segment of the inconceivable, manifold, invisible working of all upon all. Thus every human action is a vessel of infinite responsibility.

But there are men who are hourly accosted by infinite responsibility in a special, specially active form. I do not mean the rulers and statesmen ... I mean those who withstand the thousandfold questioning glance of individual lives, who give true answer to the trembling mouth of the needy creature who time after time demands from them decision; I mean the zaddikim, I mean the true Zaddik ... Men come to him, and each desires his opinion, his help. And even though it is corporal and semi-corporal needs that they bring to him, in his world-insight there is nothing corporal that cannot be transfigured, nothing material that cannot be raised to spirit. And it is this that he does for all: *he elevates their need before he satisfies it.* Thus he is the helper in spirit, the teacher of world-meaning, the conveyor of the divine sparks. The world needs him, it awaits him ever again.[129]

---

[129] Buber, *Hasidism and Modern Man*, p. 69.

CHAPTER TWELVE

Glenstal Abbey School

Did that tradition really stem from the great St Benedict of Nursia? When Benedict – not then a saint but an energetic zealot – decided to found his monastery, he chose the place on Monte Cassino because it was the site of a temple of Apollo that had survived into the sixth century of our Christian Era. Benedict's first act was to smash the image of the god and destroy his altar. Benedict was himself one of the smashers.

Did he utterly banish Apollo from Monte Cassino? He thought so, but we may wonder now if the Apollonian spirit did not live on, under the Benedictine robe. Things are never so clear-cut as even a great sage like Benedict believes them to be. Did not his sister, later known to the pious as Saint Scholastica, set up her nunnery five miles away, and meet with her brother once a year to discuss holy matters? Hindered as it was by the difficult five-mile journey, the feminine spirit still asserted itself at Monte Cassino, and one wonders whether Apollo, wherever he was, did not smile that it was so. Even Benedict could not drive femininity out of the realm of the gods, though he might banish it five miles away from his House of God.

The light of the spirit, as Apollo knew then, and probably still knows, was not the privilege of a single sex, and Benedict and his followers had to pay a heavy price because that idea never occurred to them. Nevertheless they travelled far, walking as they did, on one leg.'[130]

I n September 2012 Glenstal Abbey School marked its eightieth birthday. For a Benedictine monastery to be celebrating eighty years of anything is like Hollywood stars celebrating five years of marriage. Although it

---

[130] Robertson Davies, *Murther & Walking Spirits* (London: Penguin, 2011), pp. 276–7.

represents a mere scintilla in the vastness of history, it does offer an opportunity for assessment. I have been associated with this school for more than half its lifetime, as a pupil, as a teacher, as a principal, and so have a certain amount of experience from which to make an attempt at such an assessment.

Glenstal is situated among the foothills and forests of east Limerick, looking out over the Golden Vale to the Galtee Mountains to the south. Its deep romantic chasms and primeval oak forests were celebrated in the early nineteenth century by the construction of Glenstal Castle, built by Sir Matthew Barrington, who added to the forests by planting over one million trees, representatives of the newly discovered great botanical wonders of the world, together with some more native. The castle, in Hiberno-Norman style, is vaguely suggestive of ancient lineage and better times. Eleanor of Aquitane, patroness of troubadours, greets those who enter the door with a *Céad Míle Fáilte*, while on the other side stands a sterner Henry II. The Barringtons were clockmakers and great undertakers who arrived with Cromwell. They were generally of magnificent stature and generosity: Sir Matthew built Barrington's Hospital, Barrington's Pier, and founded a savings bank, a *Monte di Pieta* to protect people from extortionate money lenders. Sir Charles Burton Barrington helped introduce rugby to Ireland.

The grounds at Glenstal were designed as an earthly paradise. Some of the family even travelled to America to bring back trees, which are now among the largest of their type on this side of the Atlantic. Matthew's son, Sir Charles Burton Barrington, was born in 1848 and succeeded to his father's estates in 1890. This was a troubled time for such landlords. Tragic circumstances caused the estate to change hands. His daughter Winifred was in love with Captain Biggs, an English Black and Tan officer who was being targeted by local freedom fighters. On the evening of 14 May 1921, Winifred and Biggs were returning to Glenstal by car from Kimealta. They were ambushed at Coolboreen and both killed.

Sir Charles and Lady Barrington with the rest of their family left Glenstal to live in England on their Hampshire estate. They had already lost their Irish income generating tenanted land in 1911 under the Encumbered Estates Act, and may have wished to consolidate their affairs. Nothing could be done about their properties here until after the Civil War (1922–23) when Sir Charles offered it to the Irish Free State government as an official residence for the Governor-General. If the gift had been accepted, the President of Ireland might be living in Glenstal castle today. However, the offer was turned down as the estate was thought to be too far away from Dublin.

In 1926 Glenstal Castle was bought by a local priest, Monsignor James Ryan, and given to the Benedictine monks from Maredsous in Belgium to found a community there. Why were they invited? Two Murroe-born clergymen, John Harty, Archbishop of Cashel, and Richard Devane, professor of Church History at St Patrick's College, Thurles, wanted to find some appropriate future for the Glenstal Castle and estate which would also benefit their diocese and home parish. They admired the influence of Benedictine monasteries on the continent and especially Mont Cesar at Louvain and the Abbey of Maredsous in Belgium where they knew the Abbot of the time, who was an Irishman.

Why did they come? Essentially because of Columba Marmion, born in Dublin on 1 April 1858 to an Irish father (William Marmion) and a French mother (Herminie Cordier). Joseph Aloysius entered the Dublin diocesan seminary in 1874 and completed his theological studies in Rome. He was ordained priest in 1881. His dream was to become a missionary monk in Australia, but he was won over by the liturgical atmosphere of the newly founded Abbey of Maredsous in Belgium, which he visited on his return to Ireland after his ordination. In 1886 he entered Maredsous as a monk and became their third abbot in 1909.

He died in 1923. It was in his honour that the monks of Maredsous founded a monastery in Ireland, dedicated to Saints Joseph and Columba.

The archbishop who invited the monks made it clear that he expected them to start a school in the monastery. In a letter dated 8 December 1926, he wrote to the Abbot of Maredsous: 'With special pleasure, I give the community permission to establish a Benedictine house, at Glenstal, in the archdiocese of Cashel. This permission extends to an arts and crafts school, which would be a great boon to ecclesiastical art in Ireland, and also to a higher school of general students, in which Irish students would hold a prominent place.' The founding charter of this school was pretty specific. Its purpose was to provide a suitable alternative for families who were sending their boys to England to be educated and to offer Catholic education of the highest quality to those perceived to be the future of this country. On 19 January 1928, at the inauguration of Glenstal Priory, Archbishop Harty gave the blessing and told the assembled guests that he had several personal reasons for rejoicing on that day: 'I see a religious community established in my native parish; I see the Irish flag displayed on these buildings; but above all, I rejoice to see the reintroduction of the famous Benedictine Order into Ireland.' He ended by reiterating his hope that the monks would establish a secondary boarding school which would have a great social influence on the future of the country.[131]

The secondary school for boys was opened in September 1932. Father Columba Skerret OSB was the headmaster, and there were just seven boys on the roll. However, the real founding father of the school was Fr Matthew Dillon OSB, who served as headmaster twice, from 1937 to 1948 and from 1953 to 1961. During his first term of office he increased the number of boys from less than twenty to over

---

[131] Mark Tierney, *Glenstal Abbey, An Historical Guide*, fifth edition (Glenstal Abbey Publications, 2009), pp. 43–7.

100. He formed the ethos of the school and gave it its characteristic stamp. His personal influence created the unique atmosphere of the school which endures to this day.

This particular blend of education is marked by its own very specific history. At the beginning of the twentieth century in Gorey, Co. Wexford, an unusual monk from Downside Abbey in England, Fr John F. Sweetman, set up a school called Mount Saint Benedict, to provide education for young men in Ireland who might normally have gone to school in England. He was an almost fanatical Irish nationalist and did not accept the legality of the Free State government as it was not sufficiently autonomous and 'Irish'. In his school everything was unusual. Sometimes the boys got up at 6 a.m. in the morning, other times they stayed in bed until 11 a.m. Sometimes they had formal classes, more often they went picking apples for the day. Education was random and unpredictable. Sean McBride was educated there, as was Matthew Dillon, brother of James Dillon, the famous orator politician, both of whom were sons of John Dillon, the last leader of the Irish parliamentary party. Among the alumni of 'The Mount', as it was called, was D. J. Murphy, who became headmaster of St Gerard's School, Bray, Co. Wicklow, which also tried to perpetuate a similar educational tradition.

Matthew Dillon became a barrister and then joined the community at Glenstal Abbey. When he was asked to take over the fledgling school in 1937, five years after it had been started, it was 'the rugged independence, sporting respect for the freedom of others, and spartan authenticity' he had learnt at 'The Mount' that were to remain his guiding principles and inspiration. A sometimes rather gruff and abrupt manner hid a good-humoured idealism with a personality that gave to young people freedom both from 'worldly vulgarity and from the integrist piety of the age'. In his five-minute introduction to the school given to the new boys in 1959, for instance, he made a clear distinction between the moral law and school law. One need have no scruples if one breaks the latter, but 'God help you if you get caught'.[132]

From a boys' point of view he had something of the figure, the reputation and the presence of Captain Bligh, as played by Charles Laughton in the earlier version of the film *Mutiny on the Bounty*. On his ship he brooked no interference. Parents who left their children on the first day of term were advised not to contact them 'until the full horror of the place had sunk in'. These were the days when full control was possible. There was no television, The Beatles were still babies, and it was easier to phone Moscow than Murroe.

Father Matthew referred to everyone as 'Mr' or 'Dr', which excused him from having to learn their first names. But all mothers were referred to as 'Madam'.

On one occasion, a mother leaving her child in his care, on a grim September evening, insisted on seeing the bed where her precious would spend the night. She was shown a dormitory housing sixteen iron beds. 'These beds are not aired,' she said. 'Now I insist that at least one hot water bottle be put in that bed before my son gets into it.' 'Madam,' came the icy reply, 'you can choose between having your son in the bed or the hot water bottle, but they certainly won't be there together.' She decided not to press the point.

On the way down stairs she kept up the conversation: 'My boy is a very good boy. He has been very well brought up, and I don't think you are going to have any trouble with him'. 'Madam,' again came the reply, 'I do not anticipate having any trouble from the boy, but I do anticipate a great deal of trouble from his mother.' Later in his career, he offered to found a school in Iceland where there would be no interference whatever from parents.

Despite his abrupt manner and autocratic tendencies – running all aspects of school life single-handedly, except for

---

[132] Anthony Keane, 'Remembering Fr Matthew', *Glenstal Newsletter* 3 (Autumn 2006).

sport, which he left to Fr Peter Gilfedder – he was a capable tyrant and scrupulously just in his dealings with the boys. He left behind him two short treatises on education which give an account of his views on the subject:

> A parent who preferred his own judgement to that of the family doctor would be universally blamed, and rightly so ... [t]he schoolmaster, on the other hand, must expect constant interference from the parent ... It is not wise to exercise our authority to forbid everything that we think undesirable; we must recognise that children have rights and that sometimes those rights entitle them to do things which are silly. For example, it may be prudent to see that a boy is restricted to a reasonable amount of pocket money, but we should not control the way he spends it. He will probably waste a good deal of it, but that is a very good way of learning the value of money. His function is to watch as unobtrusively as possible the boy's struggle with the various problems which life presents to the young and wait for the opportune moment to intervene. Unwanted advice is seldom followed and, if we are too eager to guide, we may be suspected of wanting to control, which is almost sure to be resented. A boy of sixteen or seventeen is very jealous of his independence and may even persist in conduct which he knows to be foolish rather than appear to submit to what seems to him to be unwarranted interference ... I feel that children should be given the maximum of freedom and that supervision should be regarded as a necessary evil to be reduced to a minimum and abolished for the older boys.[133]

---

[133] Dom Matthew Dillon OSB, *Some Problems of Parents & The Schoolmaster, Parent and Pupil* (Dublin: Clonmore & Reynolds, 1950), pp. 14–25.

Fr Matthew reigned supreme from what he called 'his lonely perch'. Freedom was the order of the day, but if things got out of hand, then he would 'deal with the situation' himself. He was the only person in the school who could administer corporal punishment, which he did in the confines of his study. This solemn ritual kept the whole school in awe of him.

At this formative stage of one's schooling, the capacity to be alone, as Winnicott defines it,[134] was essential to the adolescent, because it meant that he could feel sheltered and protected as he explored his own possibilities and the world around him. A child feels that he can be alone in himself because someone else is there who asks 'nothing but to be there functioning and protecting at the border of the invisible'. Only the individual who has developed the capacity to be alone in this way, by internalising or creating such a 'protective environment', is constantly able to rediscover the personal impulse. This discovery of the personal impulse is probably the greatest single benefit which any school can confer.

Between them, Fr Matthew and Fr Celestine Cullen were thirty-seven years out of the eighty in the driving seat, the first for nineteen years and the second for eighteen, representing almost half the time the school has been in existence; the other half is covered by no less than ten headmasters, each serving between four and seven years at the helm. Father Celestine had been a boy in the school under Fr Matthew and he continued the formula outlined by his predecessor without much change. When the latter was dying he was visited by his protégé who thanked him for all the advice he had given him after he had taken over from him as headmaster. 'Advice rarely taken' was the quick reply.

---

[134] Donald W. Winnicott (1965), 'The capacity to be alone', *The Maturational Processes and the Facilitating Environment* (London: Hogarth/Institute of Psycho-Analysis). Reprinted from *International Journal of Psycho-Analysis* 39 (1958), pp. 416–20.

I was meant to take over from them and continue the dynasty for a third generation, having been a boy in the school under both of them. My quarrel was with the business of 'flogging'. I believed that this was wrong both for the boys and for the person administering the punishment. I drew up a plan, with the help of others in the monastery, for running the school without corporal punishment. I agreed to take on the job as headmaster if this plan were introduced. At first they agreed and then they backed down and said it would be impossible to run the school without this traditional method of keeping order. There was no way that a castle full of boys could be controlled without some form of punishment that they really feared. I was told that I was to start in September, acting as headmaster of the school in the way it had been run for the last fifty-five years. I refused and then was told that I would have to leave the monastery if I did not do what I was told. Obedience was the fundamental rule of a monk. I began making preparations to get a job elsewhere and to leave Glenstal Abbey. Eventually, the abbot of the time relented. Another monk was appointed headmaster and I was put in charge of the kitchens.

Five years later my point of view was adopted and there was no longer any corporal punishment in the school. Many regret this decision and believe that an important lynchpin of school discipline was removed and that an effective option was withdrawn from the school population without any consultation of their preferences.

Discipline is never a problem when people are doing what they love to do. In fact the word has both meanings: 'order maintained among schoolchildren ...' and 'branch of instruction or learning'.[135] When people are learning something they really want to learn and when the teaching is stimulating and effective, there are never problems of discipline. It should be possible in a small school to provide

---

[135] *The Concise Oxford Dictionary*, new edition, 1975.

each person with whatever they need to develop, whatever special interest and particular talent they may have. If such a service is rendered and if the possibilities for realising this goal are provided adequately, then there will be little danger of unruliness because each person will be engaged with developing themselves fully in the way they find satisfying.

The advantage of boarding school is that we have the other six hours of the day to concentrate on the rest of our humanity. There should be for every child in our school the perfect place to exercise the gifts that God has given: sport, art, theatre, poetry, nature, music, computer technology, communications, debating, journalism, broadcasting, not just here inside the school but in the areas around the school. Our job in a boarding school where the boys are here twenty-four hours a day, is to spot the talent and then have the imagination to find the place and the means whereby this talent can flourish. We need to nurture people who can move effortlessly between the arts and science, between technology and design, between creative writing and business. We need to open a space for experimentation at every level. Each child should have every opportunity to explore every possibility available. There is no end to their talent and to the variety of their skills. We have to make sure that they develop fully and totally at every level, the physical, the emotional, the intellectual, the intuitional and the spiritual.

The community in Glenstal have made some radical changes to the school they inherited, which, hopefully, make it a better place. The first is a recognition that parents are the primary educators and that unless a thriving partnership is developed between parents and those working in the school, there is little hope of successful education for the students. At least half the success story of Glenstal Abbey School is the enthusiastic and generous involvement of most parents in the total project. Parents are with us at every stage of the process and are behind us in every aspect of our endeavours on behalf of their children.

Outsiders may – sometimes do – think that this is a school where wealthy people send their children to be rid of them for as much of the year as possible. I know from forty years of personal experience that the opposite is true. Most of our parents have to make considerable sacrifices to send their children to our school. And they do it because they want the best for them. And the best is about love, understanding, imagination and trust, before it is about points or examinations, although these are also mightily important.

The second change is a recognition that not every child is suited to boarding school life and that it is vital for all concerned to make sure that only those boys who will benefit from what we have to offer should be admitted to the school. Too many people have been damaged by boarding school life because they were forced into it without their consent. We have been made painfully aware over the years that there were boys who were unsuited to boarding school of any kind. These are often somewhat introspective children who are allergic to living cheek by jowl with large groups of other boys. School life can be a misery for them and can damage them irretrievably. This is why we introduced what we now call the 'live-in'. The live-in allows the boys who might come to the school to spend some days in the summer months in this environment with the potential classmates.

At eleven years of age most children have a shrewd intuition about where they would like to go to school and whether a boarding school is an experience they would relish. But they have to want this and to choose it for themselves. At the click of your fingers you can organise twenty-two others to join you in a game of football during break on the terrace. Normal families are not geared towards total concentration on the needs of adolescents. Much of the day is spent catering for other realities and the children have to wait their turn for attention. In boarding school, everything on the timetable, from the time you get up to the time you go to bed, is organised for the benefit of the school population. At the end of the live-in we ask each one of the candidates to tell us frankly whether they themselves would like to come to this school a year later. Some of them say they can't wait to get here. Others are diffident and a few say that under no circumstances would they choose to be away from home. Parents would be foolish to try to force such a child to undertake six years of estrangement.

We are often asked: How do you answer critics of exclusive schools like Glenstal who have small-sized classes, when other schools have such huge class sizes and such poor facilities? Is this not supporting privileged and preferential education in lieu of equal opportunity for all? In my view, the possibility of real education is slim.

In Calcutta, where a friend of mine, David Mulcahy, has just opened a school for 300 children, there are said to be anything from 50,000 to 250,000 children living on the streets, according to the annual report of the United Nations High Commissioner for Human Rights.[136] The 300 chosen excludes the vast majority and in no way guarantees that those chosen will be educated. Should he not bother then to open such a school because it is not fair on the others? In my view, if even one person in the world is truly educated it will make a fundamental difference to humanity. And, in any case, education is always a mystery and a miracle. The most privileged school can be a disaster for those who cannot cope, for whatever reason. Only those who are suited to boarding school benefit from the experience; many sensitive souls are destroyed by being forced to attend. In fact, wherever you are, unless you meet the right person, education can pass you by. Geniuses can be educated anywhere by anyone under any circumstances. Picasso, when asked how to improve the teaching of art in France said: 'Give them rotten conditions and let the teaching be bad, bad, bad!' It is a matter of luck – but if the environment

---

[136] Published 11 January 2012.

is small and the atmosphere cherishing then there is more likelihood that more people can be educated.

Our view is that such realisation of the full potential of every child is more likely to happen in a small dedicated environment where each person feels recognised, understood and encouraged. If such environments are more expensive to run, then so be it. Those who believe in such opportunities for their children are prepared to forego other luxuries in favour of this vital possibility for their children. Such conditions make for optimum educational growth although never guaranteeing that eventuality for every child involved.

Other more vast and impersonal situations increase the possibility of neglect and underperformance for many students. And if, as people do say, this is a privileged education, then we say that it *is* education and anything less than this is not. If it is not possible to provide this privilege for every child in this country, then at least let those who want it, who cherish it, and who can afford it, take up the offer. Equality of educational opportunity should not mean that no one in the country should be educated in case they might have an unfair advantage over the rest.

The advantages to education in a place like Glenstal are so simple that they should be available to every child in a small country like ours. In education big is not necessarily better and 'small is beautiful'. In the 1960s when the optimum numbers game was invented, the then minister for education was holding forth on 800 being the optimum number for a secondary school at the same time that the minister for agriculture was proposing the same optimum number for pig farms. Both of them were probably misguided. Economic viability was the criterion, and it was all about electricity, infrared lamps, farrowing boxes and feeding units. The arguments came from 'educationalists' elsewhere. They haven't changed since they were first put forward:

- Education is a commodity which should be made available to all.
- No discrimination should be exercised; all have this right and therefore all must be educated.
- A comprehensive school is necessary to provide every kind of opportunity to every kind of child who must be taken in; such a school needs to have a sixth form of at least 120 pupils to make such a variety of choice possible; on average it takes a comprehensive school of over a thousand pupils to produce a sixth form of this size.
- Economically, it is impossible to provide such facilities in any more than a few strategically placed centres to which all available students from that catchment area can be ferried. We should therefore centralise our resources and make these available to all.[137]

Since this argument was elucidated in the 1960s the practicalities of its incarnation have been tried and found wanting. The most obvious mistake is at the level of human rights. There are many kinds of 'right' which have to be treated in different ways. The right to education is rather like the right to love and be loved. Although we can state that everyone has this right, we cannot prescribe what that right involves or the form it may take. Education is not a commodity which can be distributed effectively to anyone who attends a central and highly efficient, streamlined service station. Education can not be delivered like parcels in the post. The way it is processed is different for every single child.

Everything should, therefore, be scaled down to the proportions manageable by young people who are finding their way. There is more likelihood of education in a small rural school than in a custom-built complex at a distance. It

---

[137] Cf. Robin Pedley, *The Comprehensive School* (London: Penguin, 1963).

is of no educational benefit to the emerging child to be moved out of a cherishing, intimate and familiar environment to some distant location wasting time insulated in a vehicle, no matter what kind of resources or facilities are provided at the location to which they are transported. Children of this age group, and especially those going through the traumatic years from twelve to eighteen, need more than anything else an intimate and human-sized environment.

Minister for Education, Ruairí Quinn, has this to say about numbers in classrooms: 'Studies show that the quality of teaching is more important than smaller class sizes in terms of shaping educational outcomes.'[138] This reads like a conversation from *Alice in Wonderland*. The minister is not comparing like with like. He might as well say that oranges are more important than lemons. His statement compares two things which should not be brought together in an either/or situation. It is impossible to say, and the minister quotes no studies to confirm his statement, which is 'more important': quality of teaching or size of classes. Both are equally important. And, of course, no one would disagree that 'quality of teaching' is of the utmost importance but so is the number of pupils in any one classroom. The underlying implication here is that if the teacher is good, it won't matter how many are in the class. This is not so. No one can develop genuine educational contact with more than twenty pupils at any one time. It is a nonsense to say that quality of teaching is more important than class numbers. This is trying to bamboozle us into a false choice, creating an artificial antithesis that sounds plausible. As if we were forced to come down in favour of one or the other whereas we should be demanding the coexistence of both. These things cannot be compared, nor are they available for value judgments. Reduction of numbers in classes and

---

[138] Ruairí Quinn, 'The Future Development of Education in Ireland', *Studies* (Summer 2012), 101.402, pp. 130–1.

improved education of teachers are both priorities which must not be neglected.

Meanwhile, the job of each school is to fine-tune the formula in such a way that anyone who comes has a very good chance of flourishing there. Whatever the pupils do, whether they eat or play or practice or are taught, they should be developing their talents and their personalities and absorbing values, which we as parents and as educators share about what it means to be a human being, and what fosters health, well-being and happiness in our lives.

The essence of our kind of education is that everyone involved in it knows everyone else personally. As headmaster of the school, I knew by name and in person every boy, his parents, every teacher, every person working in the school in whatever capacity, and it is that fragile and delicate network which makes up the fabric of genuine education.

In my own personal experience here at Glenstal Abbey School, over the last fifty years, I have found that the stage is a magic place of education where I have seen countless numbers of very timid, insecure, unprepossessing adolescents transformed into unrecognisable maestros, as they stepped onto the boards and acted or sang a part. The most rewarding experience is when we wrote the play and the music ourselves and the cast from the school put it on for the first time. During such projects there can occur the most creative relationships between all those taking part, stage-hands, actors, electricians, directors, musicians, and it doesn't matter what age you are, what class you are in, what size you are, or what qualifications you have – everyone is equal and everyone is depending on every other person to come up trumps. And, invariably, they do. Such, to my mind, is the template for all educational systems. People working together generously and altruistically to create an environment where everyone can grow up together.

The particular charism of our school is essentially linked with its monastic ecology. The monastery provides an overarching stability and reassurance. There is another life being lived beyond the miniature world of the school. Others are standing around like oaks in the forest with other things on their minds. This is consoling without being cloying and many of the boys return to the monastery long after they have left school to seek advice or find out more about the life that was lived around them.

And it is in this context that our religious ethos can be mentioned. The monastery which surrounds the school derives its very existence from faith in the transcendent mystery of God as the source of all that exists and as the meaning of human existence. The Benedictine tradition is based on the Rule for monks written around 530 AD which provides the vision by which our lives are organised. The cornerstone of every monastery and of all monastic life is humility. For some 1,500 years, the rule of Benedict has been training people to this humility which allows us to place all our desire before God so that the Holy Spirit can point out to us where it is our own will and how it can be trained to do the will of God. This is an extension of the Jewish tradition to which we also belong: putting our lives and ourselves at the service of God's kingdom. And so a monastery is a suitable place for the special humility of the educator to be made manifest. Listen to what Dostoevsky says about the monks of Russia over 100 years ago, three months before his death:

> Fathers and teachers, what is a monk? Among the educated this word is nowadays uttered with derision by some people, and some even use it as a term of abuse. And it is getting worse as time goes on. It is true, alas, it is true that there are many parasites, gluttons, abusers and arrogant hypocrites among the monks. And yet think of the many humble monks there are who long for solitude and prayer in peace and quiet. These attract less their attention, and how surprised they would be if I told them that the salvation of Russia

would perhaps once more come from the monks. In their solitude they keep the image of Christ pure and undefiled, and when the time comes they will reveal it to the wavering righteousness of the world.

Look at the worldly and all those who set themselves up above God's people on earth, has not God's image and God's truth been distorted in them? They have science, but in science there is nothing but what is subject to the senses. The spiritual world, the higher half of man's being, is utterly rejected, dismissed with a sort of triumph, even with hatred. The world has proclaimed freedom, especially in recent times, but what do we see in this freedom of theirs? Nothing but slavery and self-destruction.

The monastic way is different. I cut off all superfluous and unnecessary needs, I subdue my proud and ambitious will, and with God's help I attain freedom of the spirit and with it spiritual joy!

Which of them is more capable of conceiving a great idea and serving it – the rich in their isolation or those freed from the tyranny of habit and material things? The monks are reproached for their solitude but it is the rich not the monks who live in isolation.

In the olden days, leaders came from our midst, why cannot it happen again now? The salvation of Russia comes from the people ... Therefore, take care of the people, and educate them quietly. That is your great task as monks, for this people is a Godbearer.[139]

When it is said that 'this people is a Godbearer', what is meant is that out of every population, certain people are called by the Holy Spirit to lead us out of bondage and into freedom. The task of the truly humble educator is to stand in the temple until such people are presented to us and then,

---

[139] *The Brothers Karamazov* (London: Penguin, 1969), Vol. I, Book 5, pp. 288–310.

like Simeon and Anna, to have the humility to recognise the one so much greater than ourselves we are called to educate. Not everyone, of course, is called either to be such a person or to recognise them, but the special humility of the educator is to be aware of that possibility and to allow for that potential in every child who is placed in our care.

St Benedict, in his *Rule*, says:

> We are, therefore, about to found a school of the Lord's service, in which we hope to introduce nothing harsh or burdensome ... but using discretion, the mother of all virtue, let us temper all things so that the strong may have something to strive after, and the weak may not fall back in dismay.[140]

Such a school should find the tempo of each and every one of the learners and begin the process wherever they happen to be. But if the person is called to more than this, then the sky is the limit and the humility of the educator is to recognise the special vocation of each one and find the means whereby each can appropriately answer that call and realise their full potential.

The monastic tradition stems from a time before many of the divisions which currently divide Christianity. Those who are in the school are aware that the monks pray four times a day in the church and that they celebrate the Eucharist every day of the year. We would hope that our way of life and our forms of worship would not be inimical to any Christian person as these derive from the earliest traditions of our common heritage. As for those in our care, we require of them to attend the Sunday liturgy of the Eucharist. Other than that we try not to impose upon anyone devotional practices or formulations of belief which we happen to find nourishing and satisfying. If there are seven billion people on the planet at this time then there must be seven billion

---

[140] *Rule of St Benedict*, Prologue and the end of chapter 64.

ways of connecting with God. Each generation, as, indeed, each individual person, will find their preferred way of maintaining such contact.

We believe in the Holy Spirit, the Lord and Giver of Life. This Spirit will lead each one of us to correct worship of God, which is the meaning of orthodoxy. After all, it is not our love for God which is the most important thing, it is rather God's love for us. The liturgy is the primary source, the *culmen et fons*, of our worship and, we hope, always open and available to all people of good will. There can be no indoctrination, no propaganda involved in education. We can give an example of the beliefs that inspire us, and give an account of the hope that sustains us to those who ask, but we can never force anyone to live their life according to the way in which we live ours, no matter how convinced we may be of its validity.

What eventually leads towards God in this situation is the special magic of the place, the spirit of the monastery, the dedicated and caring humanity of the staff, the comparatively untrammelled freedom provided, and the one-to-one contact of genuine educational relationship, all of which have made this into a place where people can grow at their own pace into the contours of their own particular personhood. Such an atmosphere is not just provided by the people who live in the monastery or work in the school, it is dependent upon the local community. Glenstal Abbey has been blessed since its beginnings by many local families who have worked tirelessly and generously to support and maintain it. It is no exaggeration to say that without such extraordinary and devoted people, the monastery as it is now would never have survived. These families and personalities are too numerous to mention by name but they are all around us, and for over three generations have been the mainstay of the monastic community's existence in this place.

The essential element in our educational process is quality contact between small groups of students and inspirational teachers. These latter have been employed outsiders or members of the Glenstal Community itself. Again the names are too numerous to mention but the number of inspirational and dedicated people who have given their lives to working in our school is not just the reason for its success but the proof of its credibility. People only give their lives to something in which they believe and which gives them evidence of worthwhile results of their efforts.

To foster such genuine educational relationship it is necessary to keep numbers relatively small. Although our school began in 1932, before there was free secondary education for children in this country, the formula devised is still valid. The philosophy of 'small is beautiful' still holds for every educational establishment catering for children up to the age of seventeen or eighteen. A school needs to be an intimate environment where everyone knows everyone else. Teaching is essentially communication between persons and there is a maximum number of pupils in a classroom which can allow real education to take place. Unless genuine educational relationship is established there is no real education as such.

Exactly twenty years ago, the then minister for education, the late Séamus Brennan, introduced a green paper called 'Education for a Changing World'. He wanted it to convey a fundamental reality that has to be confronted by all of us:

> Ireland is undergoing some of the most rapid changes in its history and is doing so in a world of ever-accelerating change. The speed of change which will continue and even increase, is being caused largely by the creativity and enterprise of people in the developed countries. In the industrialised countries, wealth is now mostly created from invention, innovation, brain power and knowledge. A nation's health is limited only by the imagination and enterprise of its people, and not by its natural resources.

He wanted 'to provide balance and breadth in education by emphasising science, technology, enterprise and creative and critical thinking:

> I want the education system to play its full role in the development of the nation's people. I want the system to lead change into the next millennium, not simply to follow it. But I want to build on the education system's existing strengths and achievements. I have no desire whatever to narrow the focus of education to purely utilitarian aims. Education must continue to embrace the moral, spiritual, physical, aesthetic and intellectual development of students.[141]

So he proposed that the 800 schools then in existence be brought down to 400 through closures and amalgamations.

In my view he should have doubled the number of schools rather than halving it. I cannot accept that any equipment, machinery, facilities, resources or buildings provide an adequate substitute for intimate and imaginative educational contact in a small environment. Children should not have to be careful that they are not run down by traffic in the corridor outside their classroom.

The ages twelve to eighteen must be one of the most difficult periods of evolution for any of us. We all have personal experience of what can happen to people in these age groups. We are aware of just how difficult many adolescents can be. Little Emperor syndrome is an expression which has been coined with reference to 'only children' in the People's Republic of China, where since 1978 most families have been restricted by law to having one child only. Without siblings, children are the sole focus of parents' attention and benefit from increased spending power and the parents' desire for their child to experience

---

[141] Seamus Brennan, T.D., Green Paper: *Education for a Changing World* (Baile Atha Cliath: Oifig an tSolathair, 1992).

the benefits which they themselves were denied. Described as a problem 'so acute that it is changing how society functions', the Little Emperor syndrome has grown beyond a side effect that 'the architects of China's one-child policy could never have foreseen'[142] into a 'behavioural time-bomb'.[143]

Greatly improved purchasing power coupled with excessive pampering causes hugely increased spending on only children. From toys to clothes, parents shower their child with material goods and give in to their every demand; it is not uncommon for children to be the best-dressed members of their families. Recently, it is not uncommon for nearly half a family's income to be spent on the child.

Little Emperors also bear the burden of heavy expectations. From an early age parents push their only child to educational extremes as they cater to their whims. Many of these precocious children can recite the English alphabet and read newspapers in traditional Chinese by the time they are ten years old, but still their parents perform basic tasks for them, fixing their hair, tying their shoes, making their beds. Despite this attention there is tough competition, as only 2 per cent of the Little Emperors will be able to study at a university. The 'four-two-one family structure' refers to the collapse of the traditionally large Chinese family into four grandparents and two parents doting on one child. The combination of immense pressure to excel and extreme pampering results in the stunting of social and emotional growth. Such perceived maladjustment of the Little Emperors has become an exaggerated topic for media reportage: stories depict children hanging themselves after being denied sweets, and cases of matricide in retribution for a scolding or a dinner served too late. All this can seem exaggerated or far away, but many can read our

---

[142] Andrew Marshall, 'Little Emperors', *The Times* (29 November 1997).
[143] Louise Branson, 'China's Brat Pack', *Sunday Times* (19 June 1988).

own situation with lack of control of adolescence writ large. This Little Emperor syndrome is a possibility for each and every one of us.

The mind of a newborn child, according to Freud, is completely 'id-ridden', a mass of instinctive drives and impulses which require immediate satisfaction. In the beginning we are amoral, selfish and unable to take 'no' for an answer. We have been described by the more cynical observers of our humanity as 'an alimentary canal with no stopper at either end.' W. B. Yeats puts it in an early poem: 'I am I, am I; ... All creation shivers/With that sweet cry'.[144]

Jung had a more positive view of the 'Ego' as necessary for the maturation of identity. It was the means whereby a child builds up and develops self-respect. Early megalomania should be knocked out of most of us by the sharp edges of real life. The child learns that 'I' am not the whole of reality, that 'the real' is not a circumference around me; that I am not the centre of the world. Such natural lessons de-centre without destroying the ego – we learn to link our ego to a larger reality by lowering the volume and switching the lights away from the ego itself.

Megalomania, however, as we see in Little Emperor syndrome, as an unrealistic belief in one's superiority, grandiose abilities and even omnipotence, is not always off the menu, as many of us have experienced to our discomfort on some occasions, in ourselves or in those closest to us. It is characterised by a need for total power and control over others, and is marked by a lack of empathy for anything that is perceived as not feeding the self.

This most difficult time for every child, as they move from childhood to adulthood, is moulded by the rough and tumble which makes up the life of every peer group and is often the most appropriate way of coming through it. It can be traumatic and one or two can be damaged by the kind of bullying which is sadly often a part of it; but the logic of life

---

144 W. B. Yeats, 'VI: He and She', *Supernatural Songs*.

and the law of the jungle, which have to incorporate a certain preparation for survival, require us to endure a certain transformation in the crucible of society. We have found over the years from tested experience that the best treatment for teenage transition is provided by the pressure cooker of the peer group. Of course there are children who are constitutionally incapable of surviving any boarding school experience, but we try to pick out any child who we think might be unable for boarding school life before they arrive. At the live-in, all these boys stay here for a few days to meet the other boys who happen to arrive and who will be their constant companions over the next six years. It may be different and more difficult when they do arrive, but their initial instinct is usually true, and by the time they reach sixth year they are nearly always agreeing with each other that it has been a positive and encouraging experience. They carry one another from unbearable selfishness and insecurity when they arrive, to genuine goodness and sociability when they leave, each respecting the other's talents and strengths with a healthy dose of humour and realism.

It is essential to encourage initiative and teamwork and not simply individual achievement. We need to nurture people who can move effortlessly between the arts and science, between technology and design, between creative writing and business. We need to open a space for experimentation at every level. Every child should have the opportunity to explore every possibility available. There is no end to their talent and to the variety of their skills. We have to make sure that they develop fully and totally at every level, the physical, the emotional, the intellectual, the intuitional and the spiritual. Our job is to spot the talent and then have the imagination to find the means whereby this can flourish.

The final point with which our present community begins to take issue with their predecessors is that, in principle, we would approve a move towards co-education.

To begin with, girls could be included in a day-boarder option without too great a need for structural adjustment. Later, a more ambitious building programme for adequate co-education facilities might be undertaken. Co-education is a fraught topic, even within our own community. However, after much debate we seem to have decided in principle in its favour, even though implementation of this decision might be a lengthy and costly process.

The argument in favour as I understand it is as follows: as a species we happen to divide in two, male and female, and it is therefore our lot to stick together through thick and thin. There could have been much more variety attached to the phylum – there are other species which enjoy a host of different varieties. But the fact is that we are two, and however much we enjoy or regret this arrangement it requires of us to cohabit the planet. Highly informed reports about the disparity of intellectual and emotional growth between boys and girls at secondary school level fail to convince.

Whatever the losses, dangers or difficulties, they seem to be outweighed by the gains, and whatever the dangers they are minimal in comparison with the benefits. The arguments put forward to support unisex education, that girls develop more quickly than boys from the ages of twelve to eighteen, that our sexual urges are too strong at that age to prevent teenagers from having intercourse or at least from being distracted from their studies, that adolescence is better negotiated in an all-boy and all-girl environment, all pale into insignificance when faced with our common destiny, which is to live together for the rest of our lives.

And so, in principle, we would now favour a move towards co-education as a more balanced and appropriate educational milieu. We believe that such a move is necessary, to make possible the best educational environment for the future.

CONCLUSION

The Disciple
The way was rocky. Lighting and mountain fire
Zigzagged around them like trembling branches.
The boy's step grew weak and ever more timid
The old man walked as always, straight and firmly.

The blue eyes gazed dreaming into his own,
And through the narrow cheeks beat the shame,
The mouth was set as from repressed weeping,
The great longing of a child came.

Then the master spoke: from much wandering
I took the gold might of the one truth:
'If you can be your own, never be another's.'
And silently the boy walked in the night.[145]

Of course, I don't have all of the answers, and education has to continue, whether we like it or not, every day of every school year; we cannot send the whole school population away until we have had time to devise the most appropriate educational programme for them. My intention has been to lay out arguments as clearly as I can so that discussion can enhance the ongoing debate, which is never definitive in this ever-changing area.

Why should I be the one to set the ball rolling? Because I happen to have had a privileged education myself and have been studying this problem for the last forty years. I taught in a secondary school for twenty of those years, I did a

---

[145] Martin Buber, *Gleanings*, in *The Philosophy of Martin Buber*, p. 40. This poem was written by Buber in 1901 when he was twenty-three. He included it in his *Nachlese* (1965) as one of those gleanings 'which appears to me today as a valid expression, worthy of surviving, of an experience, a feeling, a decision, yes even of a dream.' It was based on a quotation from the sixteenth-century Paracelsus: *Alterius non sit qui suus esse potest* ['If you can be your own, never be another's'], and it sums up the kind of relationship which he calls 'genuine educational contact'.

doctorate in the philosophy of education and taught the course in that same subject to the Higher Diploma of Education students at Mary Immaculate College, Limerick, for the course run by University College Cork. If I am unable to articulate the issues involved, then who can? It is said that it takes a fool to write the history of the world so that the experts can come later and pick holes in it. Well that is what I hope: let those who understand the situation better than I put me right. For the present I stand over the argument which I have articulated to the best of my ability here.

Just as we have to enter this world through the human body of another person, so this confusing world has to be mediated to us by a human person. Education is being led out into the world by a teacher who has learnt how to make this connection. The teacher is a human person with enough imagination and humility to know what parts of this wonderful world are likely to open the door for us into our own personhood. Becoming a person means entering that space between us and the world around us. Education means nothing less than creative encounter with the precise person who can unlock that door. The essential argument can be stated in one sentence from Martin Buber: 'Relationship educates, provided that it is genuine educational contact.' Let me state as clearly and as accurately as possible what is meant by the words 'genuine educational contact'. It means the exercise of a certain kind of influence which is not domination, and which requires the respect of the being of the pupil, as someone on the way to the independence of genuine personhood.

The work of education, therefore, can never be that of imparting a vision or supplying a 'worldview'. There is a real world out there which is more than my vision or my perspective on it. There is a child who is about to enter that world and who may be the one to provide us all with an insight never before imagined. The genuine educator is one who makes that introduction, that connection, without second guessing the conclusion or pre-empting the possible result. Anything can happen when personhood meets the universe.

The other half of this equation concerns the teacher. No one can educate without some energy or inclination to do so. Without the will to teach there is no point in embarking upon this profession. However, if the motivation is some energy other than the genuine will to educate, then the activity performed will not be education.

Those who teach must be careful that their motivation is not some desire to dominate or enjoy the students. The teacher, because of the educational situation, has a certain power over the student. This is good if it is used correctly; it is evil if abused. It is good if it helps the student towards full realisation of his or her potential and appropriation of his or her ownmost form of being; it is evil if it turns into a depersonalising force which stunts the growth or the freedom of the pupil.

In education this power can be used as a magnet and a stimulus. It helps to draw the pupil up and out. It gives a security and a strength necessary at a time when he or she lacks sufficient strength of their own to develop fully their own originality and personality. If it is exercised legitimately it is the most potent and effective way of transforming unformed being into mature being.

As in all relationships, education requires the participation of two people. On the one hand, it requires the gentle exercise of influence by the teacher, who must establish a trust and gradually confirm the pupil in his or her own being. Such a genuine relationship must at all times be true, which implies unfaltering in confrontation and tender in defeat. On the other hand, this influence must be received by the pupil in a way that allows him or her to freely incorporate it into their own life so that it becomes part of their uniquely original and organic growth. It must never be alien or imposed. Any lived relationship is refractory to the structure of abstract logic and verbal definition, which does not make it inexpressible. It means that we must find the way to express it.

In Ireland at this time we have to recognise the difference between providing education for a small select group and providing it for everyone. My argument is that even though we should allow everyone access to primary and secondary education, this privilege should take place in small environments and with one teacher for every fifteen pupils.

The whole island could be harnessed to the education project as a hedge school. Surrounded by magnificent coasts and beaches, these could become settings for learning about biology, ecology, geography, geology. Similarly, the beautiful country estates throughout the island could become settings for environmental exploration and artistic self-expression. Modern technology makes it possible to introduce children to every aspect of wildlife in these places. Nor should this prevent any of the children from being literate or numerate. On the contrary, it should be an incentive to them to perfect these skills and their own capacities to enjoy every aspect of the world they will live in.

A template for education which uses imagination as its key could promote creativity as the single greatest asset of our people. This does not mean that we downgrade or sideline any of the necessary aspects of education which include literacy, numeracy or science, it means provision of another essential element which develops the whole personality of the child and enhances every aspect of what they do in school in an imaginative, holistic and creative way. Holistic maturation of the child could be less costly and more effective than anything ever before envisaged. Inspired teaching opens the imagination, so that the living of life becomes an 'art' in itself. The educational relationship allows us to find the ability to relate not only to ourselves but to all life around us.

The image should be oil, which infiltrates and lubricates already existing structures and organisations. There is nothing preset about the paradigm. Introducing inspirational and imaginative teaching is not the answer in itself; it is the way to get to the answer. In each area and at each different time imaginative education has to be custom designed to fit the local profile in the up-to-date times and circumstances which prevail. We believe that the child (both in the classroom and as the 'child' in the adult) is key to the regeneration of our community, and thereby society, for this twenty-first-century Ireland. An 'inspired education' programme would surely augment the existing professional development of a teacher, by complementing their teacher training programmes (and later in-service courses) with experiential workshops in personal creative development, in ways that would deepen the connection of their whole person with the 'source' of the creative spirit, latent within every human being. If this became the template for education in Ireland, we could become the envy of the rest of the world in terms of our people, who would be the most imaginative, creative and integrated persons, simply because they will have been put firmly in touch with their own creative source.

I think we have to agree that the curriculum devised for primary schools dating back to 1971 has been an overall success story. Obviously it can be improved and the teachers can be better trained to cope with it. But we should not start to panic and regress to methods of the past in the interest of better literacy and numeracy. In the present economic crisis it is too easy to cut off all subventions for the arts in schools and to concentrate attention on what are referred to as 'the basics'. Such a short-term and pragmatic decision will be seen as counterproductive in the end. The full flourishing of the children in our care, in every aspect of their personal lives, including their ability to read and to calculate, should be the overall goal of our education system.

The Leaving Certificate examination and the points system for entry to university must be changed and revised. Of course it is difficult to know how best to examine and assess 20,000 students every year and to allot places in different courses at third level. And we have to agree that the points system was at least fairer in terms of gender equality and prevention of cronyism or favouritism, which teacher assessment might cultivate. But the disadvantages and the downside far outweigh any practical ease or comparative facility afforded those with the job of making the assessment. Another approach and a better system must be put in place as soon as possible.

Education must be of the whole person. It must take account of all three levels of our brain as well as catering adequately for physical, emotional, intellectual and spiritual development.

William Shakespeare, the great combiner of all three brains, has hardly been surpassed in his treatment of this subject, especially in his last play *The Tempest*, where Prospero represents the neocortex, Ariel the limbic system, and Caliban the old serpentine brain. The play takes place in the symbolic setting of an island but it represents each one of us. Prospero is each of us as ruler of our own island and in search of harmony in our lives. The two strange creatures who inhabit the island with Prospero are Ariel and Caliban, the first representing 'spirit', the second representing 'flesh'. Prospero's daughter Miranda represents the new humanity that can come from such a combination. The famous quotation: 'How beauteous mankind is! O brave new world/that has such people in it', is hers. But this brave new world is a human world. When asked about Miranda: 'Is she a goddess?', the reply is very definitely: 'Sir, she is mortal.'

Shakespeare is telling us that the new humanity, the brave new world, is not achieved by either rejecting or conquering ourselves. We have to free the Ariel in ourselves, the creative spirit, the limbic mythic system, but also we have to assume the Caliban, the serpent brain, the monster of the flesh. The whole island was Caliban's by Sycorax, his mother, until Prospero took it from him. Prospero imprisons him and treats him as 'a poisonous slave, got by the devil himself'. 'Filth as thou art,' Prospero addresses him, 'I have used thee with human care, and lodged thee in mine own cell, till thou didst seek to violate the honour of my child.'

Eventually Prospero is led from this condemnatory stance to understand that in order to restore peace to the island, to his own territory, to his own humanity, he has to take a different attitude to what Caliban represents: 'This thing of darkness I acknowledge mine,' he confesses. 'Set Caliban and his companions free/Untie the spell.' The voyage of life, which leads us through the necessary and painful tempest of the title, to the discovery of our own reality within the island of ourselves, is essentially a dialogue between all three persons of our triune brain. Prospero represents the educator. The island full of bewildering sights and noises which Caliban experiences as totally confusing, can to the eye and ear of Prospero, because of his greater maturity and experience, be interpreted as 'clear signals from a different order'. The role of the educator is to prevent us from running away from the crazy sights and sounds of the world like howling Caliban and to help us to develop 'new powers of attention and perception capable of orchestrating this mad music'.[146] The play ends:

> O, rejoice
> Beyond a common joy, and set it down
> with gold on lasting pillars. In one voyage
> Did ... Prospero [find] his dukedom
> In a poor isle; and all of us ourselves
> When no man was his own.

The job of the teacher is to help each one of us to find 'our dukedom in a poor isle', the island of ourselves, and to find ourselves when no one of us was really our own. If this happens to our children then our future and theirs will be assured.

---

[146] Alan McGlashan, *The Savage and Beautiful Country: The Secret Life of the Mind* (New York: Hillstone, 1966), p. xiii.